A Practical Primer on Theological Method is no dull look at how we do theology. It is an entryway into the multi-dimensional conversation at the heart of reflecting on theology with clarity. Bringing a tone of humility and conversation to the task, it will lead you to reflect on how you think about God, Scripture, culture, and the fullness of the creation we live in, and invite you to enjoy the Table of voices it takes to help us grow in our appreciation of God and his world.

> **Darrell L. Bock**, executive director of cultural engagement and senior research professor of New Testament studies, Dallas Theological Seminary

There are many books on systematic theology, but not many that could be considered genuinely appropriate for a beginning student. This book fills that need by introducing the study of theology in a way that is accessible, interesting, and winsome. It does not come from an eccentric viewpoint but tries to be open to many streams of orthodox Christian theology. This means it will be useful to students who don't even know yet what tradition they identify with. And there are many such students in today's Bible colleges and seminaries. If you are looking for a book to give a young, aspiring theological student, this would be a wise choice.

> **Craig A. Carter**, professor of theology, Tyndale University College

A Practical Primer on Theological Method is an accessible and well-informed introduction to the study of theology. Though designed as a text for introductory courses in theology, it could profitably be read by adults in a Sunday education program as well. It will be particularly useful for students in Christian colleges who often wonder how the study of Scripture and their faith relates to all the other subjects they are studying.

> **William A. Dyrness**, senior professor of theology and culture, Fuller Theological Seminary and author of *Modern Art and the Life of a Culture: The Religious Impulses of Modernism*

This book concerns a critical subject—how to think through the wildly different theologies on offer today. It shows the perils of thinking that *sola scriptura* could be *solo scriptura* where w[...] consensus on doctrinal and moral issues. [...] toward that great tradition, I recommend [...]

Gerald McDermott, Anglican chair [...]

Kreider and Svigel have achieved that almost impossible *via media*, a primer that is neither too technical nor too easy, a theological text in which all strands will find a welcome. With visual signposts and digestible prose, they invite readers into the broad and beautiful world of theological method. This text prepares students to enter the theological conversation with knowledge that cultivates confidence and breadth that encourages humility. I'm eager to put this into the hands of the burgeoning theologians in my classroom.

Amy Peeler, associate professor of New Testament, Wheaton College

Theology matters for every Christian. In recognition of this basic tenet of the faith, *A Practical Primer on Theological Method* offers an approach to biblical teaching and Christian belief that is both fresh and sound. Blending lively prose with robust doctrine, this volume is one I will recommend widely and enthusiastically for years to come.

Karen Swallow Prior, author of *On Reading Well: Finding the Good Life through Great Books* and founding member of The Pelican Project

This well-crafted handbook is full of solid, wise, and practical Christian guidance for Christian students in theology. I hope and pray that it will encourage many earnest disciples of Christ to pursue, study, and practice the knowledge of God in his Word and in his world.

Douglas A. Sweeney, dean and professor of divinity, Beeson Divinity School

A Practical Primer on Theological Method flouts the proverbial social wisdom not to discuss religion during dinner and instead encourages us in Table God-talk. Theology is discourse about God, and a good conversation will include voices from a number of disciplinary fields, each of which has a seat, and a voice, at the Table. Doing theology also requires table manners, virtues that keep the conversation appropriately critical and constructive. So pull up a seat as Glenn Kreider and Michael Svigel set the Table for a nourishing meal. Watch and learn as they serve up the various sources, norms, and tasks—the main courses of which the feast of theology consists.

Kevin J. Vanhoozer, research professor of systematic theology, Trinity Evangelical Divinity School

I am very excited about the work Glenn and Michael have done here, and for its potential to help Bible-believing Christians to think through and discuss theology in a meaningful and impactful way. Their integrated method and structure of content is accessible without being shallow and deep without being esoteric.

Todd J. Williams, president, Cairn University

Theological investigation often fails to reflect on the methods utilized or to acknowledge participants in the pursuit. For those considering theology anew, Kreider and Svigel provide a much-needed reminder that God's pervasive revelation compels discourse from all corners of creation. Even more, their strategic metaphor of fellowship around the Table casts a vision for how this discussion can be constructive by drawing on the strengths of multiple perspectives. This book is a gift to the guild, and every aspiring and practicing theologian needs this text as a (re)orientation to the foundational ideas of sound theological method.

Mark M. Yarbrough, professor of Bible exposition, vice president for academic affairs, and academic dean, Dallas Theological Seminary

The passion of Glenn Kreider and Michael Svigel is for evangelicals to pursue theology with excellence. *A Practical Primer on Theological Method* successfully engages the novice by treating theological method as a conversation between eight characters. On the basis of their discussions of virtue, science, or art alone, one would be required to grant this book high marks. But these wise and humble teachers have a great deal more to say. I cannot recommend this volume highly enough—take up and read!

Malcolm B. Yarnell III, research professor of systematic theology, Southwestern Baptist Theological Seminary and author of *The Formation of Christian Doctrine* and *God the Trinity: Biblical Portraits*

A
PRACTICAL
PRIMER ON
THEOLOGICAL
METHOD

A PRACTICAL PRIMER ON THEOLOGICAL METHOD

TABLE MANNERS FOR DISCUSSING GOD, HIS WORKS, AND HIS WAYS

GLENN R. KREIDER AND
MICHAEL J. SVIGEL

ZONDERVAN
ACADEMIC

ZONDERVAN ACADEMIC

A Practical Primer on Theological Method
Copyright © 2019 by Glenn R. Kreider and Michael J. Svigel

ISBN 978-0-310-58880-1 (softcover)

ISBN 978-0-310-58884-9 (audio)

ISBN 978-0-310-58881-8 (ebook)

Requests for information should be addressed to:
Zondervan, *3900 Sparks Dr. SE, Grand Rapids, Michigan 49546*

Cover design and art: Studio Gearbox
Interior design: Kait Lamphere

Printed in the United States of America

HB 11.27.2023

*Though many teachers, colleagues, and friends
have influenced us over the years as we worked out
our theological method with fear and trembling,
we dedicate this volume to Dr. Craig A. Blaising,
who set us on the path toward methodological clarity.*

CONTENTS

PREFACE

To write a primer on anything is a challenging task. By styling something a "primer," we allege that it's an elementary textbook or basic introduction to a subject; in this case, to theological method. But as any of our colleagues know, the subject of theological method is not a simple one. "Elementary" can quickly collapse into "over-simplified," and when we seek to write an "introduction," we can wind up slipping into a "superficial treatment." Acknowledging the challenges, what we're presenting in the following pages is, we hope, somewhere in the "Goldilocks" zone—not too hard, not too soft . . . just right.

Additionally, publishing this primer is tricky. Our intention has not been to say in simpler words and fewer pages what others have said in complex jargon and multiple volumes. Nor is our goal merely to survey the landscape of theological methods and let beginners know what's out there. There's a place for such books in a theologian's library, but this is not that kind of book. In this book, we're not presenting patristic method, or medieval method, or protestant method, or evangelical method, or enlightenment method, or biblicist method, or conservative method, or liberal method, or Baptist method, or covenantal method, or dispensational method, or Thomist method, or Anglican method, or any other provisional method. Rather, we present what may be called an *integrative theological method in the classic Christian tradition*. We suppose that if all of the distinct approaches to theological method were to be averaged out, the result would not be a bland, vanilla method but an approach to theology composed of the unique colors, flavors, scents, and textures of a variety of historical and contemporary theological methods. This is what we've tried to accomplish in the short space of this small book.

? FAQ

What Is a Primer?

A primer (rhymes, oddly, with "trimmer," not with "timer") is defined as "a small introductory book on a subject." As such, an effective primer should equip a reader who is completely unfamiliar with a particular field of study with the basic information needed to advance to more technical works on a topic. A primer serves as a step stool to the bottom shelf.

To this end, we've made a conscious attempt to interact with the insights and perspectives of theological traditions sometimes much broader than our own. We are confessedly "five-sola" Protestants with an obvious affection for Augustine, Calvin, Edwards, and the broadly Reformed tradition. But we don't shy away from drawing from patristic, medieval, and modern-era authors where their theological fruits are sweet or their words nourishing. And though we are twenty-first century American theologians, we are deeply indebted to the ideas of men and women from past generations, who have lived in remote parts of the world, spoken different languages, and lived out their theology in cultural contexts very different from our own—as well as those living out their Christian convictions in a variety of cultures throughout the world today.

We know that colleagues from our own institution and churches—not to mention from other institutions as well as varying theological traditions—won't necessarily see eye to eye on everything we've presented in this volume. That's unavoidable. However, we trust that in these pages we've given all of us things to think about and to talk about. We ask that the seriousness of the issues we present in this volume won't be rejected because of the chosen format of a "practical primer" for popular audiences. We also ask that readers approach this primer with the tone of voice with which it is intended—as a conversation *starter*, not a conversation *stopper*; as a conversation *continuer*, not a conversation *killer*. We invite not only the critical friendship of supporters of our approach to theological method but also the friendly criticisms of detractors.

CONTENTS AND FEATURES

The introduction and chapters 1–3 form the theological, philosophical, and methodological foundation of this book. They should be read with care. Chapters 4–11 constitute the heart of the book, each chapter focusing on a vital perspective necessary for a well-balanced approach to theological discourse. Chapter 12 concludes the book with a brief summation, an illustration, and an invitation to join the fellowship of saints engaged in theological discourse. Complementing the main text, you'll encounter several features:

The **Centerpiece** feature provides the basic thesis of each chapter in one or two short sentences. If you ever forget what the chapter is about or what we're arguing, refer back to the centerpiece at the beginning.

FAQs will call attention to frequently asked questions that come to us from students or colleagues. Though these questions—and many more—are addressed in the main text as well, we believe certain common questions deserve brief, succinct answers to aid in clarity. Sometimes these FAQs will define key terms or underscore important concepts in the chapter. For definitions of other unfamiliar terms, we recommend consulting a theological dictionary.[1]

The **At the Table** sidebar in chapters 4–11 indicate several of the intersecting fields of inquiry and study that make up each seat at the Table. These are only examples. Some of these fields fit into more than one seat, indicating the interdisciplinary nature of theological method. More thorough definitions or descriptions of these fields can be found through various online or print resources.

The **Taking Your Seat** feature gives us opportunities to highlight practical implications and applications from each chapter. In this

---

1. E.g., Gregg R. Allison, *The Baker Compact Dictionary of Theological Terms* (Grand Rapids: Baker, 2016); Matthew S. DeMoss and J. Edward Miller, *Zondervan Dictionary of Bible and Theology Words* (Grand Rapids: Zondervan, 2002); Donald K. McKim, *The Westminster Dictionary of Theological Terms,* 2d ed. (Louisville: Westminster John Knox, 2014).

sidebar, we directly address our readers, urging specific changes of mind, attitude, or actions. We'd like for readers to take their time with this feature.

At the end of each chapter, we drop in on the **Jerusalem Council** to see how the principles of the Table were addressed to a specific doctrinal and practical issue in the apostolic church. This gives a biblical example of theological method in action.

In addition, you will find a handful of charts and diagrams to help illustrate the text. In all cases, these diagrams should be interpreted by the text itself, which explains the purpose of the images. Images are great tools for retention and organization, but if they are interpreted apart from the text they are intended to illustrate, they can lead to great misunderstanding.

ACKNOWLEDGMENTS

We want to expressly thank a number of our colleagues, students, and first readers who contributed to our own exploration and articulation of theological method—both prior to, during, and after the writing of this book:

To our friends and students, Mike Bauer, Christopher Crane, Nancy Frazier, Kevin Gottlieb, Dani Ross, Andy and Sandra Stanley, Torey Teer, and Dean Zimmerman, and to our colleagues at Dallas Seminary, Carisa Ash, J. Lanier Burns, Garland Dunlap, John Dyer, Sandra Glahn, J. Scott Horrell, Elliott Johnson, Shannon Reibenstein, Josh Winn, and Timothy Yoder, who provided helpful critical feedback on early drafts of the book.

To fellow scholars, theologians, ministers, and teachers whose comments, questions, and critiques improved the project immeasurably: Michael Bird of Ridley College, Sean B. Bortz of Cumberland University, Craig Carter of Tyndale University College and Seminary, R. Todd Mangum of Missio Seminary, Jonathan Master of Cairn University, Gerald McDermott of Beeson Divinity School, David Moore of Two Cities Ministries, Ken Stewart of Covenant College, Justin Taylor of Crossway, Jon Marq Toombs of Christ Covenant Church, and Kevin Vanhoozer of Trinity Evangelical Divinity School.

INTRODUCTION

AROUND THE TABLE

Centerpiece

Theological method can be likened to a round Table discussion among several intersecting fields of inquiry all centered on God's revelation.

A round Table in the corner of a cozy lounge seats eight personae.[1] Each figure personifies a field of study comprised of countless men and women from every nation, tribe, language, and people reaching far back in history. To be sure, they are a diverse and ever-changing cast of characters, but don't be distracted by the participants in the discussion. Instead, we need to focus on the thing that has captivated the eyes of anyone who has entered this hallowed hall. At the center of attention is the light of God's threefold living revelation: the Word to the World, the Word in the World, and the World of the Word.

Who happens to be seated at the Table tonight?

The World of the Word . . . The Word to the World . . . The Word in the World

---

1. Because the characters in this metaphorical illustration represent fields of study, inquiry, or unique approaches to encountering God's revelation, there is no gender-specificity or ethnic identity implied in these personae. Both women and men from any cultural or ethnic background function in each of these fields. This Table is open to anyone.

The Word to the World: God's verbal revelation, primarily in Scripture, including his message through prophets, angels, and other verbal means

The Word in the World: Jesus Christ, the incarnate Word, and the body of Christ, the church, as the Spirit-indwelled mediators of his mission

The World of the Word: Everything created by God, through his eternal Word, by the Spirit, things visible and invisible

---

Peering through the top of his bifocals, the balding *Interpreter* wears a red sweater over a collared shirt. If he were to slouch in his chair (which he never does), he would disappear behind a stack of lexicons, grammars, and commentaries, one of which he recently wrote himself. Ready at hand to assist him stand Old and New Testament specialists, textual critics, linguists, exegetes, and lay readers—both experts and non-experts with a love for God's Word, ready to lend a hand in the careful study of God's verbal revelation.

? FAQ

Doesn't "the Table" make theology about talking and sitting rather than doing and going?

We agree that theology isn't an end in itself. Theology should be in the service of life, ministry, and mission. Our analogy of the Table can be taken too far, especially if we picture theological method as just sitting around a table jabber-jawing about theoretical or esoteric concepts while the believer-on-mission can't wait to get up, walk out, and do *real* ministry. The Table is just a teaching tool. We could have used the image of a starship crew going "where no one has gone before" if our emphasis were on the outward-focused mission of the church. Or we could have employed a platoon of soldiers on the battlefield if our emphasis were on the apologetic nature of the Christian faith. For our purposes, the Table works to represent the historical and contemporary community of faith gathered together for mutual edification.

To the Interpreter's right tonight sits the *Theologian*, wearing a cardigan sweater because her office is usually chilly, eager to offer knowledge and insight on the art of "faith seeking understanding." Her focus is on Christianity's Great Tradition—the ancient and enduring center, story, and standards of the faith.[2] She labors over both the unity and diversity of what has been believed, taught, and confessed in the various Christian churches and denominations worldwide. Behind her is an auxiliary of fellow theologians—both professional and nonprofessional—prepared to help in the quest of better understanding, explaining, and communicating God's revelation and how it all fits together in a unified whole.

To the right of the Theologian sits the conscience of the Table, known simply as the *Virtuous*, dressed in a crisp white-collared button down shirt and a classic blazer. She's a paragon of goodness and beauty, renowned not only for her faith, love, and hope but also for her prudence, temperance, fortitude, and justice. Her entourage of assistants from every continent and era includes those with expertise and experience in contemplation, morality, spirituality, aesthetics, and ethics. For millennia they have strived to grasp God's revelation not only with the mind, but also with the heart and hand, applying its truth to the purpose of transforming lives.

Next comes the *Philosopher*, draped in a classic mantel as if he just stepped out of Raphael's *The School of Athens*. He's surrounded by classic and contemporary books on epistemology, metaphysics, hermeneutics, aesthetics, logic, philosophy of religion, ethics, and other dense volumes. His supporters ancient and modern, Western and non-Western, have spent their lives deep in thought—reading, writing, and conversing among themselves in pursuit of a better understanding of the three facets of God's revelation.

Leaning back in her chair this evening, directly opposite the Interpreter, sits the *Scientist*. She is dressed in a white blouse and even whiter lab coat. She smiles thoughtfully as she thumbs through a scientific

---

2. As we will explain in chapter 5, "The Task of the Theologian," the Great Tradition of Christian orthodox theology consists of the *center* (Christ's person and work), the *story* (the Trinitarian creation-fall-redemption narrative), and the *standards* (church confessions, universal creeds, doctrinal statements, and classic ordinances).

journal, jotting down notes. Behind her swarm numerous representatives of the hard and soft sciences—physics and chemistry, astronomy and biology, sociology and psychology, even computer scientists and engineers—all applying their interests and expertise to the exploration of God's revelation.

Sporting a Bob Dylan t-shirt under his black sports coat, the *Artist* concentrates on the pencil sketch he's creating, trying to capture nuances of the subject that can't be reduced to words. After a few minutes, he sets down his pencil, strokes his beard, and leans back in his chair, tipping it onto its rear legs. He listens to his fellow artistes and artisans from every culture and every era, who are gathered behind him. They're producers and performers, writers and musicians, painters and sculptors; men and women skilled in the creative and fine arts. Also among them are scholars of culture, including popular culture. In dramatically diverse ways, they have strived to grasp and express the ideas communicated through God's revelation.

Beside the figure of the Artist sits the well-groomed *Minister* with his traditional clerical collar.[3] With a binder of sermon notes, counseling tips, and other bits of wisdom accumulated through years of preaching and pastoral care, he comes to the Table with unique questions and concerns, as well as answers and insights, that many of the others don't share. His associates who have served in the same capacity across the generations include ministerial workers from a variety of social, cultural, and church backgrounds—some experts in practical theology, preaching, teaching, counseling, administration, and shepherding, all eager to continue to apply the practical implications of God's revelation.

Finally, between the Minister and the Interpreter sits the *Historian*. Dressed in a navy pantsuit that exudes both experience and

---

3. The Minister at the Table is not necessarily one who holds the appointed office of pastor, deacon, elder, or bishop, in the modern or historical senses. As will become obvious in chapter 10, "The Labor of the Minister," our use of the persona "Minister" is intended to include all believers—men and women—involved in both vocational and non-vocational ministry, as described in Ephesians 4:11–16. In this primer, we do not advance a position on which offices may be reserved for male leadership, as do many denominational standards. Christians throughout history have differed on this issue. For two contrary positions, see, The Council on Biblical Manhood and Womanhood, accessed 20 February 2018, https://cbmw.org/ and CBE International, accessed 20 February 2018, https://www.cbeinternational.org/.

expertise, she closes a recent volume on the history of the Reformation and places it on the stack of history books in front of her. Other colleagues who have contributed to her field of discipline include experts in historiography, scholars of church history, and those who labor in the history of interpretation and world history. For ages, all of them have employed their skills toward understanding God's revelation in and throughout global history.

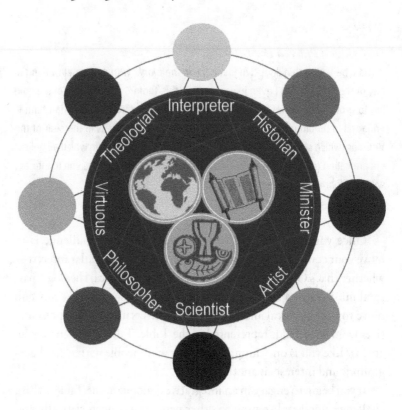

Chances are you can identify with more than one of these eight figures. The truth is, in any real-life theological dialogue, one person can simultaneously give voice to the Historian, the Minister, the Virtuous, the Interpreter, and any of the others at the Table. These aren't rigid roles, but perspectives that need to be considered, "voices" that need to be heard. Each of us is equipped with traits, talents, training, and temperament suited for unique contributions to the passionate pursuit of God's revelation. And in any case, all of us should exemplify the insights of the Virtuous and the impulses of the Minister.

Yet the Table presents us with several challenges. The first challenge is simply to decide to accept the invitation to the Table and to engage in a humble discussion concerning God's revelation. It's a high and holy calling to give your time and energy to the task of theology.

? FAQ

Do I Have a Place at the Table?

Maybe you're thinking, "I'm just a [*fill in the blank*] with no formal training in any of these fields. Do I even have a seat at this Table?" Yes! Any believer seeking to grow in his or her understanding and experience of the Christian faith is engaged in theology. Even if your normal place at the Table is in the seat of the Virtuous (which should be all believers' pursuit) or the Minister (in which all believers are called to be engaged), we hope this primer will encourage you to interact with and learn from those in other fields.

Once you've committed to it, though, a second challenge is to move your conversation beyond your own field of particular interest— whether that's Old or New Testament studies, historical theology, pastoral ministry, or a combination of several of these areas. We must all move toward a critical and constructive conversation with representatives from *other* fields represented at the Table. Talking to people who are just like you is one thing; conversing with people with other backgrounds and interests is another.

If you begin to engage in an integrative dialogue at the Table, a third challenge emerges: listening to other perspectives both critically and constructively. Not every perspective is right, not every contribution is wrong, and seldom is any perspective solely or completely right or wrong. Determining if and how each insight fits into your own understanding of God's revelation can seem like an unsolvable puzzle. But the interactions between the Interpreter and the Scientist, the Philosopher and the Artist, the Minister and the Virtuous—these are the stuff of constructive theological dialogue, as we'll soon discover.

Finally, deciding whether any of your own theological positions need to be modified, nuanced, or abandoned in light of the insights of your brothers and sisters who are seated at the Table—that's the greatest challenge. To admit that your own construal of God's revelation was incomplete, unclear, or simply wrong takes humility, wisdom, and patience. How easy it can be simply to double-down when faced with differing perspectives which may, in fact, better reflect the light of God's revelation than your own, or maybe just provide a different perspective worth considering!

66 Taking Your Seat

Consider which perspectives at the Table you're most comfortable voicing in theological discussions. Also think about which personae are most alien to your gifts, training, interests, and experiences. How might you strengthen your ability to contribute positively to ongoing theological discussion? What areas might you need to focus on and what kinds of diverse perspectives might you want to incorporate? As you build a ministry team to accomplish a particular mission, think about which fields illustrated by the Table's personae might need to be represented on your team. And as you seek to answer doctrinal or practical questions, which voices need to be invited to the Table?

Regardless of the personae with which you resonate and which roles at the Table you feel most comfortable, you're invited. You simply need to pull up a chair and join the conversation. It really is that simple.

But how? What do you say when you take your seat? Where do you start? What are the "rules" of the Table? These are the questions this primer is going to help you answer. Think of it not merely as a "how-to" manual for theological method, but a handbook of etiquette for discussions with other believers centered on God's revelation. In the following pages, we present theology's "table manners"—the manner, mode, and means of engaging in discourse concerning God, his works, and his ways.

The Table is set. Many of the invitees have already taken their seats. In fact, they've been chatting with each other for generations, even centuries. But it's not too late to get involved. God's revelation is calling to us—to *all* of us and to *each* of us. And the Spirit of God is drawing you to the Table.

Please accept the invitation.

Jerusalem Council

The Jerusalem Council of Acts 15 exemplifies the principle of Christians coming together to deliberate over theological matters. In fact, this example has been the basis for local synods, ecumenical councils, and other deliberative meetings throughout the history of the church. In each chapter of this book, we'll drop in on the Jerusalem Council to observe how the various positions at the Table contribute to theological reflection. In the final chapter, we'll draw all of these contributions together to provide a clear picture of how the Table can work.

The problem raised and settled at the council was both theological and practical. In the course of the mission to the Gentiles, some Jewish followers of Jesus began teaching, "Unless you are circumcised, according to the custom taught by Moses, you cannot be saved," and "The Gentiles must be circumcised and required to keep the law of Moses" (Acts 15:1, 5). In response to this great controversy, Paul and Barnabas headed to Jerusalem to consult with the "apostles and elders" there (15:2 NASB). The result was a kind of Table meeting to deliberate and decide.

CHAPTER 1

WHAT THEOLOGICAL METHOD IS AND ISN'T

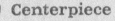

Centerpiece

After clearing up some common misunderstandings, "theological method" is defined as the manner, mode, and means of participating in discourse concerning God, his works, and his ways.

Before we can describe a Christian theological method, we need to define two basic terms: *theology* and *method*. You've probably heard it said that *theology* is "the study of God" (*theos* = "God" and *logos* = "study of"). However, we assert that a better definition of *theology* would be "discourse concerning God."[1] This not only reflects the meaning of the word itself, from *theos* ("God") plus *logos* ("word/discourse"), but it also reflects historical understanding of the *task* of theology.

What's the difference? Does it matter? Are we merely engaging in word games?

---

1. The Methodist theologian, John Miley, asserted, "The term theology . . . means primarily a discourse concerning God" (John Miley, *Systematic Theology*, vol. 1, Library of Biblical and Theological Literature, ed. George R. Crooks and John F. Hurst, vol. 5 [New York: Hunt & Eaton, 1898], 2). See also Alister McGrath, *Christian Theology: An Introduction*, 6th ed. (Malden, MA: Wiley Blackwell, 2017), 86. Of the several pages of definition for the Greek term λόγος in the standard Greek lexicon, BDAG, none of them are "the study of something," while "discourse," "exposition," or "conversation" is a viable meaning. See William Arndt, Frederick W. Danker, and Walter Bauer, *A Greek-English Lexicon of the New Testament and Other Early Christian Literature* (Chicago: University of Chicago Press, 2000), 598–601.

The phrase "study of God" summons an image of a person hunched alone over a desk, surrounded by books, deep in thought, diligently pursuing knowledge about God, his works, and his ways. On the other hand, the phrase "discourse concerning God" always envisions two or more people—a discussion group, members of a seminar, a teacher and her class, or even a writer and his readers. Further, strictly speaking, we're not studying God himself, but God's *revelation*—what he has revealed about himself. In short, we don't ascend to God and study him; we're dependent on God's condescension to reveal himself to us, in our world and in our language and symbols. As women and men engaged in theology, we respond to what God has revealed—those things that are no longer secret (Deut. 29:29).[2]

But what about the term *method*? The word actually comes from two Greek words, *meta,* "after," and *hodos,* "way, road, or path," that is, "a following after" or "a pursuit." In its common usage, it refers to a "pursuit of knowledge, investigation," or, in our sense, a systematic mode of carrying out an inquiry.[3] Depending on the nature of the investigation, inquiry, or pursuit, a method may involve principles, procedures, techniques, or rules. A method could be rigid, with deviation leading to disaster—as in following a formula for making Coca-Cola—or a method could be dynamic, with a built-in need for flexibility and fluidity—as in skillfully winning a game of chess. In any case, the "method" serves as a pair of guardrails, keeping the pursuit on the right path. It establishes the ground rules for the conversation.

So, then, what is *theological method*? Simply put, *theological method is the manner, mode, and means of participating in discourse concerning God, his works, and his ways.* The three M's in this definition tend to overlap in their conventional uses, but in our definition, "manner" refers to the attitude, disposition, or orientation toward theology; "mode" is the mechanics, procedures, or techniques of theology; and "means" refers to the sources, resources, or tools we use in theology.

---

2. By "revealed" we are not limiting revelation to the past. Christians have always believed that God continually reveals himself to humanity, which will become clear as we proceed. They have not agreed on how he does so, however.

3. See Henry George Liddell, Robert Scott, Henry Stuart Jones, et al., *A Greek-English Lexicon* (Oxford: Clarendon Press, 1996), 1091.

Throughout this primer, we use the term "theological method" to refer to the method of *systematic theology*, not biblical theology, canonical theology, pastoral theology, historical theology, or any other fields called "theology." As will become clear, all of these perfectly legitimate and necessary pursuits fall under the broader umbrella of "systematic theology," and they often have their own unique "methods." "Theological method" in this primer refers to the broadest (and most ambitious!) theological pursuit of integrating the findings of all the "ologies."

Let's try to better understand our working definition by describing *theological method* from two different angles: what theological method *isn't* and what theological method *is*.

WHAT THEOLOGICAL METHOD ISN'T

Before we explore some of the facets of what theological method *is*, let's look at four things theological method *isn't*.

Theological Method Isn't a Formula

Think high school math and the Pythagorean Theorem: $a^2 + b^2 = c^2$. Plug in the right data, and you get the right answer. Guaranteed. If you get the wrong answer, there's something wrong with your data or something wrong with you. But the formula itself? It's foolproof.

Not so with theological method.

There is no formula. There is no tried and true process; no step one, step two, step three; no secret recipe that turns raw biblical data into perfectly balanced doctrine. We have principles, guidelines, and boundaries, sure; but theological method is more like a soccer game than a scripted play; more like a conversation than a lecture; more like Coltrane than Bach.

? FAQ

What Is Theological Method?

Theological method is the manner, mode, and means of participating in discourse concerning God, his works, and his ways.

Theological Method Isn't Exegetical Method or Inductive Bible Study

One of the greatest challenges we encounter with our graduate students of theology is confusion between exegetical method, inductive Bible study method, and theological method. Many of us were taught that theology was more or less a linear process—like going from harvested wheat to a fresh loaf of bread. That approach went something like this: First, you harvest the biblical data related to the subject you're studying—say, *angels*. Look up all the verses on angels, study what each one says about the subject, and gather them together. Second, process these bits of data: analyze, organize, synthesize them. Finally, summarize the data into a final comprehensive articulation of the whole Bible's teaching on the topic. The end result, we were told, is an article of the faith—part of a systematic presentation of what the whole Bible teaches on various topics.

That's not systematic theology. And that's not the theological method we are presenting.

Rather, the above process is a vital *part* of theological method, at least much of the time. In fact, as we'll learn in this book, exegesis and inductive Bible study involve several methods essential to theological method: exegesis, biblical theology, canonical theology, and other disciplines that have their own distinct (but related) principles and practices. But these are all subsidiary parts of the broadest discipline of systematic theology.

Another challenge is the confusion between hermeneutics and theological method. If hermeneutics is "the study of the principles of interpretation," then hermeneutics is a component of theological method.[4] But hermeneutics is often limited to the interpretation of texts, particularly the text of Scripture. As crucial as the reading of Scripture is, Scripture also teaches that God has revealed himself through other means, too. And they must also be interpreted. David Jasper puts it well: "Hermeneutics is about the most fundamental ways in which we perceive the world, think, and understand."[5]

---

4. Hermeneutics is often described as a science and an art. For example, see Wayne McDill, "Seven Principles of Biblical Interpretation," *Lifeway: Pastors*, accessed 20 February 2018, https://www.lifeway.com/pastors/2014/03/12/7-principles-of-biblical-interpretation/.

5. David Jasper, *A Short Introduction to Hermeneutics* (Louisville: Westminster John Knox Press, 2004), 3.

Theological Method Isn't "Whatever It Takes to Win the Argument"

Too often "theological method" is actually a euphemism for "doing-whatever-it-takes-to-demonstrate-that-my-view-on-this-particular-doctrine-is-the-right-one." Such a pursuit does have its place; there is a "faith" that should be articulated and defended (Jude 3). At times false teachers and false doctrines need to be refuted. Moments arrive when skeptics and critics need to be answered. There's room for a focused application of reason and rhetoric intended simply to defend a particular doctrinal position—especially something that's part of the main entrée of theology—the Trinitarian creation, fall, and redemption narrative centered on the person and work of Jesus Christ in his first and second coming.

However, when theological method deteriorates into polemics—defending my view (or my specific articulation of my view) from detractors or doubters—it tends toward "food fight" rather than "table fellowship." That's the method we might follow in party politics and team sports. That's not theological method.

Theological Method Isn't Assuming What One Attempts to Prove

Some believers calling themselves "biblicists," "Bible-believers," or "exegetes" harbor a negative view of systematic theology. They sometimes accuse systematic theologians of practicing a method that simply goes to the biblical text to find support for their already-held system of theology. In this misunderstanding of theology, rather than allowing doctrines and beliefs to emerge from the hermeneutical process, the proof-texting theologian goes to the text looking for support for her conclusions.

Critics often accuse theologians of approaching the text with preconceived conclusions rather than allowing the text to frame not only the answers but the questions as well. Of course, everyone approaches God's revelation with some preunderstanding, but theological method must allow the revelation to shape the questions and listen for God to provide the answers to the questions he himself raises. No one approaches Scripture as a blank slate. Everyone believes something. Yet a proper method submits to Scripture rather than manipulating Scripture for the interpreter's purposes.

WHAT THEOLOGICAL METHOD IS

Having looked at a handful of things that are *not* theological method, we're ready to fill in our understanding by looking at five things theological method *is*.

Theological Method Is More of an Art than a Science

Not that it isn't also a "science," but in our experience the doing of theology is as much intuitive as it is methodical.[6] Lutheran theologian John Mueller writes:

> Christian theology is not a science in the same sense as, for instance, geology, psychology, biology, etc., are sciences. It differs from these sciences not only in subject-matter, but also in source, method, and purpose. Nevertheless, Christian theology may be rightly called a science if by that term we understand a *definite* knowledge, or *accurate* and *reliable* information, in opposition to mere views, opinions, and hypotheses.[7]

As an art, theological method is as creative and fluid as it is linear and logical. It involves the head and the heart, the mind and emotions, reason and reactions. It involves the whole person—heart, soul, mind, and body (cf. Mark 12:30). One learns it by doing it (and even doing it wrongly) as much as one learns it by observing others do it. And often when you become an experienced theologian, you begin to have a feel for it, and it becomes difficult to explain just what it is you're doing and why.

---

6. The term "science" is not easily defined. J. P. Moreland observes, "There is no clear-cut definition of science. Neither are there any generally accepted and sufficient conditions for drawing a line of demarcation between science and nonscience" (*Christianity and the Nature of Science: A Philosophical Investigation* [Grand Rapids: Baker, 1989], 56). Moreland also argues, "The widespread belief that there is something called *the* scientific method" is false (59). Similarly, Thomas Adajian, "The Definition of Art," *Stanford Encyclopedia of Philosophy*, accessed 13 October 2017, https://plato.stanford.edu/entries/art-definition/, writes, "The definition of art is controversial in contemporary philosophy. Whether art can be defined has also been a matter of controversy. The philosophical usefulness of a definition of art has also been debated."

7. John Theodore Mueller, *Christian Dogmatics* (Reprint; St Louis: Concordia, 2003), 68–69.

But this doesn't mean theological method is without rules or boundaries. Like any art, there are conventions, techniques, media. Think about it. Every painting has some sort of surface, every performance has some kind of stage, every symphony a score. But if we try to reduce theological method to something like the scientific method, we'll lose something critically important. Theological method is not a set of rigid steps to be followed.

Theological Method Is Dialogical

This relates to the "discourse" aspect of the definition of *theology*. Remember, we defined theological method as *the manner, mode, and means of engaging in discourse concerning God, his works, and his ways*. This obviously requires dialogue. One cannot carry on a discourse alone.

If it's deemed odd for a person to carry on a long conversation with herself, it's similarly problematic for a Christian to do theology outside of community. Proper theological method is dialogical—a focused conversation involving other people, sourced in, centered on, and structured by God's revelation.

This doesn't mean theological dialogue has no rules. Just as we can commit a social *faux pas,* people can make doctrinal missteps. And just as we can ruin relationships through toxic words, we can damage the faith by misconstruing God's revelation. Boundaries, or guardrails, protect the truth. Certain presuppositions and preunderstandings must be assumed in theological dialogue. Christian theology, for example, begins with the conviction that Christianity is true and that rejections of Christian claims cannot also be true. In short, if there is a God, then the denial of God's existence cannot also be true.

Theological Method Is Hermeneutical

Simply put, *hermeneutics* is defined as "a tradition of thinking or of philosophical reflection that tries to clarify the concept of . . . understanding."[8] Or, more simply, "the process of understanding." Hermeneutics concerns the presuppositions, principles, and procedures

---

8. Gerald L. Bruns, *Hermeneutics Ancient and Modern* (New Haven: Yale University Press, 1992), 1.

related to understanding. This could involve understanding a document, a work of art, a culture, a person, or a cloud formation. This process also requires the interpreter to understand herself and her context and situation.

Yes, theological method is an art and a dialogue—and as such, it's somewhat abstract, fluid, and—well, mushy.[9] But it's also a science of sorts. And like any science, theology has developed "binding protocols," "guiding traditions," "rules of thumb," and even "tricks of the trade." This is how it fits into the broad field of "hermeneutics."

Theological Method is Eclectic and Integrative

Because God's revelation has come to us through a variety of means, theological method must be eclectic—drawing on several pieces of information from various sources. And if it is eclectic, theological method must also be integrative—drawing together and synthesizing information. What are the means by which God has variously revealed himself to us, which we must draw together in an integrative method? In this book we categorized these broadly as the Word to the World, the Word in the World, and the World of the Word. By God's Word to the World, we mean that God has spoken and we have access to his speech in and as the canonical Scriptures.[10] By the Word in the World, we mean the incarnation of the Son of God who became flesh, came into the world he had made, and continues to indwell and empower his corporate body in the world. And by the World of the Word, we mean creation, the cosmos, the earth and the universe that God created and continues to sustain. (These three means of God's revelation will be more fully explained in chapter 3, "Three Cords of God's Revelation.")

---

9. Stanley E. Porter and Steven M. Studebaker, "Method in Theological Method: An Introduction," in *Evaneglical Theological Method: Five Views*, ed. Stanley E. Porter and Steven M. Studebaker (Downers Grove: InterVarsity Press, 2018), 5, describe the current state of theological method as "murky." They explain, "The recurring problem is that proposals on theological method, though strong on defining what theology is and why it is important, are weak on saying how to apply the method" (6–7).

10. By "Word" we mean more than the Bible. According to the Scriptures, God has spoken many words that are not preserved for us in the Bible. For example, when the Lord met with Abraham at his tent (Gen. 18), there apparently was more conversation than is recorded in this chapter. Also, John declares that what is recorded in his Gospel, and presumably in the other three, is only a small portion of what Jesus said and did (John 21:25).

We can better understand each of these means in light of the others; they mutually inform and confirm each other. They cannot be separated from one another, but they can and must be distinguished. Though God's Word to the World is entirely sufficient for making a person wise for salvation in Christ and lighting our path of godly living, it's truly understood in the context of a personal relationship with the God-Man and in fellowship with the Spirit-indwelled community of the body of Christ (the Word in the World).[11] And God's Word is received, illuminated, and lived out in the real world (the World of the Word), which also reveals God's eternal power and divine nature and, rightly perceived through illumination by God's Word, sharpens our understanding of God's revelation as a whole. In short, God's Word helps us interpret God's World, God's World helps us interpret God's Word, and the Word who came into the World is the interpretive key for all revelation.

One helpful definition that underscores the eclectic and integrative nature of theological method describes the task of theology as "collecting, scientifically arranging, comparing, exhibiting, and defending of all facts from any and every source concerning God and His works."[12] This definition is unpacked as follows: "Theology is therefore a Θεο-λογία (*Theo-logia*) or discourse upon one specific subject, namely, *God*. However, since no consideration of God will be complete which does not contemplate His works and ways in the universe which He has created, as well as His Person, theology may be extended properly to include all material and immaterial realities that exist and the facts concerning them and contained in them."[13]

Thus, theological method integrates the variety of ways God has made himself known.

Theological Method is Sapiential and Missional

The goal of a Christian theology is not merely understanding or knowledge, as important as those things are; it must also be sapiential

---

11. See 1 Tim. 3:15, where Paul reminds his protégé that this is the purpose of the Scriptures.
12. Lewis Sperry Chafer, *Systematic Theology*, vol. 1 (Reprint; Grand Rapids: Kregel Publications, 1993), 6.
13. Chafer, *Systematic Theology*, 1:1–3.

and missional. By sapiential, we mean the goal is wisdom—virtuous thinking and living in light of God's revelation. Theological method is in the service of changing our attitudes and actions, passions and priorities. The Table conversation ought to produce wise followers of Jesus, people whose lives are marked by Christlikeness, and who are equipped to go out into the world to let that light shine before others (Matt. 5:16). The mission of the church in the world is enhanced as a result of theology.

Men and women should walk away from the Table better, not bitter. They should be *trans*formed, not just *in*formed. They should be motivated to grow and go, not settle and sit. Theological method should produce mature disciples of the one who is Wisdom incarnate. Theology "forms identity and character."[14] We become like the God whose revelation is the subject of our dialogue. We know what love is because God has loved us, and we must pursue that love in community as the epitome of theological wisdom and share that love with the world as ambassadors of the kingdom of heaven.

66 Taking Your Seat

Many people have focused on theology as an individual task. The Christian reads the Bible, perhaps studies what other people have written about it, and comes to conclusions through personal study. If you've tended toward an individualistic approach to biblical and theological study in the past, consider what practical changes you can make to participate in a more table-wide discussion with others. This would ideally involve literal conversations and time spent with other believers face-to-face. Or it may involve listening to or reading the insights of other believers around the world and throughout history who bring different strengths and perspectives to the Table. Also, frequently evaluate the tone with which you engage in your theological discourse. Manifest the fruit of the Spirit in your personal conversations, discussions, and debates, whether in person, in writing, or on social media.

---

14. Ellen T. Charry, *By the Renewing of Your Minds: The Pastoral Function of Christian Doctrine* (New York: Oxford University Press, 1997), 240.

CONCLUSION

In light of what theological method is and isn't, it might be helpful to think of it in terms of a "focused dialogue." This is why we've employed a guiding illustration of a casual dinner with a variety of guests around a Table. As such, we expect structure without stricture, fluidity without futility. We have conventions and traditions, but not stifling rules and regulations. We enjoy both one-on-one conversations and table-wide discussions. And yes, because of the elbow-to-elbow, face-to-face, intermural nature of the dialogue, we'll need to moderate some squabbles, skirmishes, and even all-out strife.

But at this Table we must focus our attention on the center: God's revelation through the Word to the World, the Word in the World, and the World of the Word. We keep our hearts beating with the goal of edification and transformation, with growing and going, with ministry and mission. We recognize that this process is guided and empowered by the Spirit of God, whether or not every participant in the conversation is "our kind of Christian." As we engage in this task together, we become better skilled at the art and science of theological method—*the manner, mode, and means of engaging in discourse concerning God, his works, and his ways.*

 Jerusalem Council

When certain Jewish followers of Jesus insisted that circumcision was necessary to be saved (Acts 15:1) and that Gentile converts had to observe the law of Moses (15:5), Paul and Barnabas didn't each retreat into their studies to work out the answer as lone scholars following a scientific method. They brought the doctrinal and practical question to a council. And when the council gathered, they didn't limit their arguments to one or two sources or call on the insights of one or two experts. Peter didn't stand up and shut down the discussion with a "word from the Lord," nor did he force his own agenda as one who obviously had sympathies with those who wanted to maintain Jewish distinctions and practices.

Rather, the various members carried on a serious *dialogue* that bordered on the informal. Together they sought to understand God, his works, and his ways. The method of seeking understanding was to come together to debate (15:6–7). The *manner* was deferential, humble, and respectful. The *mode* was orderly, thorough, and integrative deliberation. And the *means* included an eclectic set of sources and information—from personal experiences in ministry to the teaching of Scripture, from the historical and cultural reality of the Jewish synagogue to the virtue of peace and unity in the body of Christ.

CHAPTER 2

REVELATION AT THE CENTER

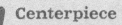

Centerpiece

Theological method centers its discussion on God's authoritative revelation, but because human discourse concerning God's revelation is always fallible and subject to correction, theology is a second-tier dialogue always in submission to God's first-tier revelation.

We don't discover God. He discloses himself.

We don't uncover data. God unveils truth.

We don't climb up to heaven. God comes down to us.

Theological method is not a method of discovery but of reception. God gives; we receive. Theological method involves faith and dependence on God as the giver, though this orientation of faith and humility may be implicit rather than explicit. Christian theologians must begin the task of theology conscious of this dependence.

Defining theology as "the study of God" confuses this relationship. We are unable to study God directly as an object of inquiry. But we can study, reflect on, and dialogue about what God reveals to us. As God told Moses, "You cannot see my face, for no one may see me and live" (Exod. 33:20).[1] But God has gone to great lengths to make

---

1. That this is a figure of speech is obvious, since God is immaterial and thus does not have a face. God's "face" apparently represents the fullness of his essence.

himself known to us, in the world where we live, the world God has created, because God really does want to be known (Acts 17:27–28).

God's revelation is the theologian's authority. Because God cannot be known unless he condescends to make himself known to us, his revelation comes with divine authority. All beliefs must conform to his truth. All actions must submit to his commands. All attitudes must be governed by his heart and mind. When a belief, attitude, or action—either our own or someone else's—deviates from God's revelation, we must listen to God rather than to humans.

Theological method begins with revelation; God takes the initiative to make himself known to his creatures. They respond, and that response is theology—our discourse about God. Over a century ago, B. B. Warfield argued:

> If God be a person, it follows by stringent necessity, that He can be known only so far as He reveals or expresses Himself. And it is but the converse of this, that if there be no revelation, there can be no knowledge, and, of course, no systematized knowledge or science of God. Our reaching up to Him in thought and inference is possible only because He condescends to make Himself intelligible to us, to speak to us through work or word, to reveal Himself.[2]

(RE)SOURCES OF (AND FOR) THEOLOGY

The Reformer John Calvin wrote, "If we reflect that the Spirit of God is the only fountain of truth, we will be careful, as we would avoid offering insult to him, not to reject or condemn truth wherever it appears. In despising the gifts, we insult the Giver."[3] In keeping with Christian thinkers throughout history, Calvin acknowledged that truth—from whatever means—is a gift from God, a blessing of God's grace toward humanity. Left to ourselves, humans will thirst for even a drop of truth. And that truth flows to humanity as a gift from the divine

2. "The Theology of Systematic Theology," *The Presbyterian and Reformed Review*, 7 (1896): 250.

3. Calvin, *Institutes* 2.2.15, in John Calvin, *Institutes of the Christian Religion*, vol. 1, trans. Henry Beveridge (Edinburgh: The Calvin Translation Society, 1845), 317–18.

fount, as the refreshing waters of truth rain on us through the Word *to* the World, the Word *in* the World, and the *World of* the Word.

Because of this, theologians speak of "sources of theology," distinct means by which divine revelation comes to us from its single ultimate source—God himself.[4] Thomas Oden defined "sources of theology" as "those varied channels, means, or conveyances by which the divine address comes to humanity and an understanding of God is thus possible."[5] Again, we recall the wise words of Warfield:

> It is with no reserve that we accept all these sources of knowledge of God—nature, providence, Christian experience—as true and valid sources, the well-authenticated data yielded by which are to be received by us as revelations of God, and as such to be placed alongside of the revelations in the written Word and wrought with them into one system. As a matter of fact, theologians have always so dealt with them; and doubtless they always will so deal with them.[6]

Because wisdom, understanding, insight, and discovery are all effects of God's grace and mercy, we understand that all revelation is truth and that all truth is revelation or a response to revelation. However, we find it helpful to differentiate between what we will call *the first-tier source of truth* (what God says and does as his revelation of himself) and *second-tier sources* (what people say and do in light of the revelation of God). God's threefold revelation of the Word to the World (available to us today in Scripture), the Word in the World (Christ and his body on earth, the church), and the World of the Word (everything that God has created) constitute the first-tier source. Every other resource legitimately employed in our discourse concerning God, his works, and his ways constitute second-tier sources.

---

4. Systematic theologies often discuss the number of sources. Most adopt some form of the "Wesleyan Quadrilateral," and then focus on how the sources relate to one another. For example, see Alister E. McGrath, *Christian Theology: An Introduction*, 6th ed. (Malden, MA: Wiley Blackwell, 2017), 104–34. As helpful as those discussions are, all revelation from God is from God; he is the source.

5. Thomas Oden, *Systematic Theology*, vol. 1, *The Living God* (New York: Harper & Row, 1987), 342.

6. "Theology of Systematic Theology," 251.

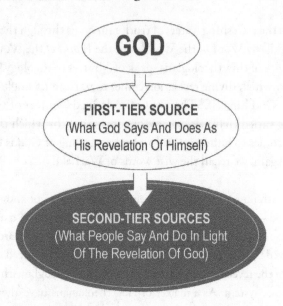

THE FIRST-TIER SOURCE OF THEOLOGY

The first-tier source of theology is God's revelation—what God says and does as his revelation of himself. This revelation comes to us by three distinct but inseparable means, which we will explain more clearly in the next chapter: the Word to the World, the Word in the World, and the World of the Word. This self-revelation must not be rejected; it must be received.

Let's use an illustration to make this clear. Open up an original Hebrew Old Testament. These words, without translation, interpretation, or commentary, are a sure and inviolable written revelation of God (Gen. 1:1):

בראשית ברא אלהים את השמים ואת הארץ

These and all other written statements of inspired Scripture—in their original Hebrew, Aramaic, or Greek texts—are God's revelation. God's revelation in Scripture (the Word to the World) must not be rejected; it must be received. And it must also be interpreted.

Now look outside your window. Better yet, step outside your door. In the midst of God's handiwork—whether perceivable or unperceivable—you are encountering an unrelenting and unimpeachable witness of

God, his works, and his ways. God's revelation in his creation (the World of the Word) must not be rejected; it must be received. And it must also be interpreted.

Now imagine you lived in the first-century land of Galilee, in the city of Capernaum. One day you hear about a man preaching about the coming kingdom of God and calling people to faith and repentance. His ever-growing throng of followers are whispering rumors that this man, Yeshua, is the Messiah. Then you see and hear him for yourself. Everything hinges on your response to him, and having seen for yourself, your responsibility is even greater. Even today, God's incarnate Son, Jesus, alive forevermore and ever-present with his people through the power of the Spirit, is the only Lord and Master to whom we owe unhesitating trust and allegiance. None of us has ever seen him, but we have heard reliable testimony from eyewitnesses about what he said and did. Those eyewitnesses recorded their testimony in the Scriptures (1 Cor. 15:5–8; 2 Pet. 1:16–18). Because of the ongoing work of the Holy Spirit, we receive what these eyewitnesses passed on to us (1 Cor. 2:9–16). And the Spirit continues to reveal the Savior through the testimony of the Christian tradition. Jesus is the revelation of perfect divinity and perfect humanity. God's revelation in Jesus Christ (the Word in the World) must not be rejected; he must be received. And he must also be interpreted.

The Word to the World, the Word in the World, and the World of the Word constitute God's threefold revelation—our first-tier source for theology. This revelation is what God says and does as his unveiling of himself.

? FAQ

But Theological Method Must Give Priority to
Scripture as the Highest Authority, Right?

It's best to talk about God and his revelation (the Word to the World, the Word in the World, and the World of the Word) as the highest authority for theology and to place our own human knowledge, words, and wisdom under God's revelation.

In chapter 4, "The Role of the Interpreter," we explain how and why Scripture has always functioned as the central norm and primary source for theological reflection. But we must resist taking this to an extreme that pits Scripture against other means of God's authoritative revelation or places an overconfidence in the ability of the fallible human *interpreter* of Scripture.

THE SECOND-TIER SOURCES FOR THEOLOGY

If the first-tier source for theology is what God says and does as his revelation of himself, then second-tier sources for theology are what people say and do in light of the revelation of God. The first-tier source always needs to be received and interpreted, and the interpreter is always fallible, limited, and stuck in his or her own limited time, space, and experiences. The result of the interpretation of first-tier revelation are our second-tier sources for theology. The second-tier sources include everything from our translations of Scripture and commentaries about Scripture to our tomes on systematic theology or volumes on historical theology. Second-tier sources can be the raw data drawn from observing God's creation or the theories developed through a careful scientific method. They may be works of visual art designed to illuminate or illustrate truth about God's creation or works of fiction intended to experimentally delve into matters of virtue and vice from a purely "under-the-sun" perspective.

The first-tier source for theology—God's own self-revelation—can never be corrected. However, second-tier sources for theology may be challenged, improved, rejected, clarified, complemented, supplemented, confirmed, and refined. The first-tier source for theology is infallible. This means that it's never subject to inaccuracy or falsehood. The second-tier sources are fallible. This doesn't mean that they are always inaccurate or false, but that they are always subject to inaccuracy or falsehood.

Now, at this point some may be thinking, "Well, if only the first-tier source is infallible, we'll just ignore the untrustworthy second-tier sources and stick with God's revelation in the Bible."

No, we won't. Because we can't. Remember, God's revelation *must be interpreted.*

The sobering truth is that our best English translation of the first-tier Hebrew text of Genesis 1:1 (the Word to the World) is subject to inaccuracy and falsehood, and the moment we open our mouths to explain what it means that God created the heavens and the earth in the beginning (Gen. 1:1), we're already uttering statements that belong to the second tier.

And if we were to imagine what the Lord Jesus (the Word in the World) would do in any given situation as a principle of Christian morality ("What Would Jesus Do?"), we're engaging in second-tier speculation about God's first-tier revelation in Jesus Christ. We may come close, and we may respond better in that situation because of this Christ-centered reflection, but we're always subject to our own frailty and folly.

When we take a high-resolution photograph of a sunset (the World of the Word), that image is a second-tier representation of God's first-tier revelation in creation. It always falls short of the original splendor of the creation itself. Even a virtual reality "experience" of creation is a fallible interpretation of the original.

In short, it's utterly impossible for finite human beings to carry on any kind of discourse concerning God, his works, and his ways except by conversing in the language of second-tier sources. Everything we think, say, or do in light of God's revelation belongs to the second tier. *Everything.*

At this point, then, you might consider adopting a model in which the first-tier source is used to correct the second-tier sources. However, if all of our reflections on first-tier sources are second-tier activities, then any such exercise is really just a dialogue between various second-tier sources. The only resolution to this dilemma is if our second-tier truth claims reflect God's first-tier revelation as faithfully as possible.

So, let's say we translate the first-tier Hebrew text of Genesis 1:1—

בראשית ברא אלהים את חשמים ואת הארץ

as

"In the beginning God created the heavens and the earth."

And let's say this translation really is an appropriately faithful rendering of the original. If so, this translation should properly function as a correction to an interpretation of God's first-tier revelation in creation that might state, say, "The universe can and will create itself from nothing."[7] In fact, even if the word we've translated as "created" were to be better rendered "fashioned," or if "the heavens and the earth" were better interpreted as "invisible things and visible things," these different renderings would still be sufficiently faithful to the fairly clear meaning of Genesis 1:1 to rule out some scientist's inaccurate second-tier proposition drawn from God's first-tier creation.

The fact is that all reflections on the first-tier source of God's revelation are second-tier sources for theology. This fact doesn't make accurate and authoritative theological reflection impossible. It simply means that theology must be seen as a dialogue—a discourse concerning God, his works, and his ways. And in this discourse, all dialogue partners are accountable to God's perfect revelation of himself and subject to correction by each other.

---

66 Taking Your Seat

Consider the potential dangers of failing to distinguish between what God reveals about himself, his works, and his ways (God's revelation as the first-tier source) and what we say about God, his works, and his ways (second-tier sources for theological discussion). If you elevate to the status of "infallible revelation" a fallible interpretation of Scripture, a fallible conclusion from science, or a fallible representation of Jesus's values and priorities, the results to theology, practice, and mission can be disastrous. Here great humility is necessary. We must always keep God's infallible revelation at the center, not our own preferences, prejudices, or pet doctrines.

CONCLUSION

By every indication we have, God wants to be known and has gone to great lengths to reveal himself. No one ever responds completely and

---

7. Stephen Hawking and Leonard Mlodinow, *The Grand Design* (New York: Bantam, 2011), 180.

perfectly to him and his revelation, but we can and must listen to him and live in light of what he has revealed.

Because the doctrine of God's revelation and the implication for sources of theology is so foundational to theological method, the next chapter will explore in more depth the Word to the World, the Word in the World, and the World of the Word. Then, in chapters 4–11 we'll discuss how each participant at the Table contributes to the conversation centered on this threefold revelation of God.

Jerusalem Council

God could have settled the question at the Jerusalem Council instantly by providing a prophetic utterance from on high through Peter, Paul, or one of the other apostles or prophets. But he didn't. Instead, God led the leaders of the church to gather and discuss the matter, leaving us an insightful record of a second-tier deliberative process centered on the first-tier revelation of God, his works, and his ways.

In this particular case, the dialogue involved apostles, pastors, and teachers— "the whole church" (Acts 15:22)—who met together and drew wisdom and insight from Holy Scripture, from personal and shared ministry experience, from core doctrines centered on the saving work of Jesus Christ, and even from historical and cultural realities. Weighing the evidence and arguments, they came to a consensus on the matter, settling the doctrinal and practical question. This is a great biblical example of a *community* approach to asking and answering theological and practical questions.

CHAPTER 3

THREE CORDS OF GOD'S REVELATION

Centerpiece

God has spoken and continues to speak to us through three interrelated means: The Word to the World, the Word in the World, and the World of the Word.

I n our discourse concerning God, his works, and his ways, we must listen and respond—humbly and eagerly—to the revelation of God. Strictly speaking, we have *one* source of revealed truth—God. Yet this divinely-sourced revelation comes to us by three distinct but inseparable means that might be pictured as a braided cord of three strands: the Word to the World, the Word in the World, and the World of the Word.[1] Let's introduce each of these in turn.

---

1. For more defense of this approach, see Carisa A. Ash, *A Critical Examination of the Doctrine of Revelation in Evangelical Theology* (Eugene, OR: Pickwick, 2015).

> **The Word to the World:** God's verbal revelation, primarily in Scripture, including his message through prophets, angels, and other verbal means
>
> **The Word in the World:** Jesus Christ, the incarnate Word, and the body of Christ, the church, as the Spirit-indwelled mediators of his mission
>
> **The World of the Word:** Everything created by God, through his eternal Word, by the Spirit, things visible and invisible

THE WORD TO THE WORLD

Scripture is the central focus of the theological dialogue. As conservative Protestants, we confess the centrality of Scripture in theological method. Scripture isn't the only means God has chosen to sovereignly and graciously reveal himself to humanity. The Bible itself describes other means by which God reveals truth or manifests his power, glory, or will—Jesus Christ, creation, conscience, angels, and visions. However, most doctrinal and practical questions that concern Christian theology—that is, anything that could be stated in the form of a question—is often *most directly* addressed in Scripture. In fact, Scripture was given expressly for the purpose of "teaching, rebuking, correcting and training in righteousness," so that believers would be "thoroughly equipped for every good work" (2 Tim. 3:16–17). And in the same context, the apostle reminds Timothy that from infancy he had been taught that the purpose of Scripture is "to make you wise for salvation through faith in Christ Jesus" (2 Tim 3:15).

In his letter to the Romans, Paul puts it this way: "But now apart from the law the righteousness of God has been made known, to which the Law and the Prophets testify. This righteousness is given through faith in Jesus Christ to all who believe. There is no difference between Jew and Gentile, for all have sinned and fall short of the glory of God, and all are justified freely by his grace through the redemption that came by Christ Jesus" (Rom 3:21–24). Scripture's purpose, then, is not to be the only source of knowledge about God but to be the source of answers for our deepest needs. The question, "How can an unrighteous person be made right with God?" is answered only in the Scriptures.

Sometimes we hear people describe Scripture as the "supreme authority" in theology or the "final authority" in matters of faith and practice. In proper contexts, these descriptions are true.[2] For example, if we were to place Scripture next to, say, a papal decree, the ruling of a medieval council, a statement by a board of elders, a report from a panel of scientists, or a position paper by a department of theologians, the inspired words of Scripture have "supreme authority," regardless of what kind of relative authority those other persons or bodies may have.

But if we place Scripture beside the revelation of God in Jesus Christ (the Word in the World) or the revelation of God in creation (the World of the Word), it would be absurd to pit these other means of God's self-revelation against each other. Whether God reveals himself through sign language, oral speech, the written word, a shade tree, or an exploding supernova, *God is revealing himself.* And every manifestation of God—clear or unclear to the observer—is true, authentic, authoritative, and binding.

An objection we hear to this is that such a position denies the doctrine of the sufficiency of Scripture, which some understand to mean that the Bible is the *only* source of knowledge about God, his works, and his ways. But this position misunderstands sufficiency. According to Wayne Grudem, "The sufficiency of Scripture means that Scripture contained all the words of God he intended his people to have at each stage of redemptive history, and that it now contains all the words of God we need for salvation, for trusting him perfectly, and for obeying him perfectly."[3] Notice several things about this definition.

---

2. Carl F. H. Henry writes, "The scriptural revelation takes epistemological priority over general revelation, not because general revelation is obscure or because man as sinner cannot know it, but because Scripture as an inspired literary document republishes the content of general revelation objectively, over against sinful man's reductive dilutions and misconstructions of it. Moreover, it proclaims God's way of redemption to sinful man in his guilty condition" (*God, Revelation, and Authority*, vol. 1 [Dallas: Word, 1976; reprint, Wheaton, IL: Crossway, 1999], 223). For Henry, God's revelation in Scripture and in creation are both true revelation. What gives Scripture "epistemological priority" is not that it is truer or clearer than revelation in creation or in Jesus Christ. Rather, the *form* of revelation in Scripture is more immediate: it comes to us in divinely inspired words ("an inspired literary document"); and the *content* of Scripture more directly addresses theological questions: "it proclaims God's way of redemption to sinful man."

3. Wayne Grudem, *Systematic Theology: An Introduction to Biblical Doctrine* (Grand Rapids: Zondervan, 1994), 127. Italics in the original deleted.

Scripture is *verbal* revelation; it describes other forms of revelation. Scripture is *progressive*; God's verbal revelation is *cumulative*. Scripture gives us what we need *for faith and practice*; it doesn't address all of our concerns. Surely the Bible helps us make wise decisions, but it doesn't directly address which house or car to buy, whom to marry, where to go to school, or even which church to attend.

This last point may bother some people who advocate an inherited "Bible only" approach to theological method. Ironically, though, the idea that Scripture alone is our *only* source for doing theology is actually indefensible in light of the Bible's own teaching! Before long, theologians sworn to the Bible alone as the sole source for discourse concerning God, his works, and his ways will find themselves in the awkward position of the Bible pointing outside itself to other sources of true and binding revelation of God, both past and present. For example, it is the Bible that commands the study of ants to learn wisdom (Prov. 6:6–8) and flowers and birds to learn not to worry (Matt. 6:25–30). Robert Duncan Culver puts the problem well: "We shall take the Bible as our guide, as usual in all matters of religious belief, but if so, then the Bible must point beyond itself to certain other sources of information."[4] This doesn't relativize or downgrade the central role of Scripture in theological method. Instead, it takes the Bible's own teaching about revelation and truth more seriously.

The proper place of Scripture in theology will be more directly addressed in chapter 4, "The Role of the Interpreter."

THE WORD IN THE WORLD

Except in certain sectarian corners of Christendom, it has always been the position of Christian theologians that God the Son, who became once and forever incarnate as the God-Man Jesus of Nazareth, is the central and supreme revelation of God: "Christ, Himself the Sum of all revelation, is Himself also the one Revealer."[5] Only by the Son is

4. Robert Duncan Culver, *Systematic Theology: Biblical and Historical* (Ross-shire, UK: Mentor, 2005), 46.

5. William Burt Pope, *A Compendium of Christian Theology: Being Analytical Outlines of a Course of Theological Study, Biblical, Dogmatic, Historical*, vol. 1 (London: Beveridge, 1879), 38.

the Father revealed (John 1:18; 14:9); and the Holy Spirit reveals the Son (John 15:26). In him all things in heaven and on earth find their unity, purpose, and fulfillment (Eph. 1:10). Arthur Holmes notes, "The entire Bible makes it clear that God's supreme self-revelation occurred in the person and work of His Incarnate Son."[6]

As the center of God's personal revelation, Jesus Christ as the Word in the World is the center and goal of Holy Scripture, the Word to the World.[7] He is also the source, ruler, and organizing principle of all creation, the World of the Word. It will be shown in chapter 5, "The Task of the Theologian," that the person and work of Christ should take a rightful place as the starting point, center point, and endpoint of our discourse concerning God, his works, and his ways.

Of course, Christ himself has ascended on high. It would be tempting, then, for us to dismiss this means of personal revelation as no longer applicable and to focus instead on the remaining means of God's self-disclosure—the Word to the World and the World of the Word. However, upon more careful reflection, we realize we are not left without God's Word in the World—a personal, in-the-flesh, Spirit-empowered revelation of God, his works, and ways. The community of saints—the body of Christ on earth—is itself a corporate revelation of God.

How so?

Ephesians 3:10–11 says, "His intent was that now, through the church, the manifold wisdom of God should be made known to the rulers and authorities in the heavenly realms, according to his eternal purpose that he accomplished in Christ Jesus our Lord." Christ is present on earth, in his body, the church. Christlikeness reveals the Word in the World, as we "grow to become in every respect the mature body of him who is the head, that is, Christ. From him the whole body, joined and held together by every supporting ligament, grows and builds itself up in love, as each part does its work" (Eph. 4:15–16).

Ephesians 2:10 declares that those who have been saved by grace through faith are "God's handiwork, created in Christ Jesus to do good works." The term translated "handiwork" is *poiēma*, the same

---

6. Arthur F. Holmes, *Christianity and Philosophy* (Chicago: InterVarsity, 1960), 14.
7. Jesus himself seems to claim this in John 5:39–40 and Luke 24:25–27, 44–47.

term used in Romans 1:20 for the things that have been made by God that clearly reveal his "invisible qualities—his eternal power and divine nature." In the Septuagint (the Greek translation of the Old Testament), the same term is used with reference to the works God has done in history: "All people will fear; they will proclaim the works of God and ponder what he has done (*poiēma*)" (Ps. 64:9; cf. 143:5). In any case, the "handiwork" of God reveals something about his character to the world—his grace, mercy, love, justice, power, and holiness. The Spirit-indwelled community of saints, as the in-the-flesh project of redemption and renewal, is an observable revelation of God, as Paul said, "What if he did this to make the riches of his glory known to the objects of his mercy, whom he prepared in advance for glory—even us, whom he also called...?" (Rom. 9:23–24).[8]

This is why Christ, who is the true Light, can by extension address his disciples as "the light of the world" (Matt. 5:14). As a revelation of God's light by our very existence as a redeemed people of God, Jesus instructed them (and us through them), "Let your light shine before others, that they may see your good deeds and glorify your Father in heaven" (5:16). Paul puts it this way, in his instructions to the Ephesian church: "Live as children of light . . . Have nothing to do with the fruitless deeds of darkness, but rather expose them" (Eph. 5:8–11).

The central place of the person and work of Christ, within the context of the Trinitarian creation-fall-redemption narrative, will be addressed more directly in chapter 4, "The Task of the Theologian." And the Spirit-indwelled body of Christ as a locus of God's self-revealing works will be teased out in greater detail in chapter 6, "The Burden of the Virtuous" and chapter 10, "The Labor of the Minister."

THE WORLD OF THE WORD

The Dutch Reformed theologian Abraham Kuyper wrote, "With a little thought one readily sees that Revelation is not merely founded in Creation, but that all creation itself is revelation."[9] Classic Christianity

---

8. See also the explicit language of corporate revelation in Phil. 2:14–16 and the body imagery of the church in 1 Cor. 12.

9. Abraham Kuyper, *Encyclopedia of Sacred Theology: Its Principles*, trans. J. Hendrik de Vries (New York: Charles Scribner's, 1898), 259.

has always accepted the axiom that creation is a revelation of God—without qualification. This includes all things visible in the physical creation as well as all things invisible, such as the spiritual realm. Beyond this, human reason, conscience, and "natural law" reveal their Creator. The World of the Word is not an "inferior" revelation, not an "unclear" revelation, not a "twisted" revelation. The world created and providentially sustained by the Father, Son, and Holy Spirit continues to pour forth clear and convincing knowledge of God, his works, and his ways.

Yet some have seen revelation in creation—sometimes referred to as "general revelation" or "natural revelation"—as inherently inferior to the revelation in the Bible. There are several reasons people see things this way. First, they are concerned that viewing divine revelation in creation as true and authoritative would undermine the importance of the Bible. Others are concerned that seeing God in creation might lead to pluralism or even universalism, as if wisdom leading to salvation by faith in Christ Jesus could somehow come from wordless revelation in creation. Still others recognize that false religions misinterpret God's revelation in creation and thus argue that the solution is to avoid interpreting that revelation at all, instead of finding proper ways to interpret it. Finally, some argue that the purpose of God's revelation in creation is only to condemn—that God gave just enough revelation of himself through the things that were made to condemn humanity.

However, the apostle Paul teaches that God reveals clear, authoritative, and illuminating truth through his creation (Rom. 1:18–25). This revelation is so clear and compelling that all who perceive it—and reject the God who fashioned it—stand justly condemned before him (Rom. 1:18). Verse 19 unpacks the logic, explaining how it is that all people could stand guilty before God: "since [or, "because"] what may be known about God is plain to them, because God has made it plain to them." How did God make this knowledge "plain" to them? The next verse explains: "For since the creation of the world God's invisible qualities—his eternal power and divine nature—have been clearly seen, being understood from what has been made, so that people are without excuse" (1:20). Note that Paul goes all the way back to an act of God—the creation of the world. However, the modifying clause, "being understood from what has been made," indicates that this revelation continues to "speak" to us in the present. And it continues to speak to us clearly, even though the creation we observe has been cursed (cf. Gen. 3:17–19; Rom. 8:19–22).[10]

What, exactly, is "understood" or "perceived" by means of this revelation through the World of the Word? Paul describes it as, literally, "his invisibles." These include "his eternal power and divine nature" (Rom. 1:20). God is not playing hide-and-seek. He's not veiling himself *behind* creation.[11] Paul elsewhere declares: "God did this so that they would seek him and perhaps reach out for him and find him, though he is not far from any one of us. 'For in him we live and move and have our being.'" (Acts 17:27–28).[12] The final phrase in this verse is important. The nature of this revelation of God's "invisibles" is so clear that all people "are without excuse" (Rom. 1:20). It is, in fact, the basis upon which wrath is revealed from heaven; it is the just cause of their resulting judgment (Rom. 1:18, 20–25).

This emphasis on knowledge of the truth appears several times in the passage. In verses 21–23, Paul declares, "Although they knew God, they neither glorified him as God ... they became fools and exchanged the glory of the immortal God for images." In verse 28, he says "they did not think it worthwhile to retain the knowledge of God." Therefore, a close reading of Romans 1:18–25 demonstrates that the creation is a true, clear, and convicting revelation of God—though a *wordless* revelation of God. The World of the Word doesn't consist of verbal statements about God, but the "truth of God" is revealed by non-verbal means—trees, stars, planets, humans, animals, air, life ... *everything.*

---

10. For helpful examples of how God is revealed in creation, see John Fischer, *Finding God Where You Least Expect Him* (Eugene, OR: Harvest House, 2003) and Philip Yancey, *Rumors of Another World: What on Earth Are We Missing?* (Grand Rapids: Zondervan, 2009).

11. This emphasis on the clarity of God's revelation of himself also helps us understand the justice in God's judgment. If the true God is clearly seen, yet we reject him or replace him with idolatrous notions of "divinity," our condemnation is completely just. If it were true that God's revelation in creation is murky or foggy, then our inability to perceive God could be an excuse for failing to honor him.

12. The specific "this" in verse 17 is God's sovereignty in marking out the nations and the places where we live, but it is introduced with the claim that God is the Creator of the world and everything in it (v. 24). In this sermon on Mars Hill, Paul never quotes from the Bible, but he does quote, with approval, several pagan poets. We will return to the rule of culture in theological method in a later chapter, "The Passion of the Artist."

Paul's teaching on the revelation of God through creation is supported by Psalm 19, which Paul very likely had in mind as he penned Romans 1. In that majestic psalm, David writes, "The heavens declare the glory of God; the skies proclaim the work of his hands. Day after day they pour forth speech; night after night they reveal knowledge" (Ps. 19:1–2). On one hand David states that the heavens "declare" God's glory and "proclaim" God's work. But these aren't literal words. This is the World of the Word: "They have no speech, they use no words; no sound is heard from them" (Ps. 19:3).[13]

Based on Romans 1:18–25 and Psalm 19:1–3, classic Christian theology has accepted the World of the Word as clear, compelling, and convicting nonverbal revelation from God. God's revelation through creation is as authoritative for discourse concerning God, his works, and his ways, as is God's revelation through the Word to the World and the Word in the World. In fact, at times some questions that come up in theological discourse will be answered primarily by exploring God's revelation in nature.

? FAQ

Why Don't You Just Use the Categories of "General Revelation" and "Special Revelation"?

The terms "general revelation" and "special revelation," though common among modern theologians, have proven to be confusing and even misleading categories. This terminology answers the question, "What is the scope of this means of God's revelation?" The answer: "It is general," meaning "given to all people at all times" or "it is special," given to some people at some times. However, many hear "general" and "special" and think they mean "common" versus "superior," "vague" versus "specific," "fuzzy" versus "clear," or "ordinary" versus "extraordinary." Because of these misunderstandings, we will not be using the terms "general revelation" and "special revelation" as categories for theological method.

---

13. See also the psalmist's declaration that the earth is full of God's unfailing love (Pss. 33:5; 119:64).

THE UNIQUENESS OF THE WORD TO THE WORLD

At this point, you might be wondering, "If God has revealed himself by the Word to the World, the Word in the World, *and* the World of the Word, is there anything distinctive about the Scriptures?" Paul answers that question, too, in Romans 1. The gospel reveals the righteousness of God—how an unrighteous person can become righteous (Rom. 1:16–17). Salvation is by grace alone through faith alone (cf. Eph. 2:8–9), and this message is the only hope for sinners. Because all have rejected God's revelation in creation (Rom. 1:18–32), and because "all have sinned and fall short of the glory of God" (3:23), only the gospel can solve the problem of sin (3:21–22).

In his second letter to Timothy, Paul reminds his son in the faith that from infancy he had been taught that the Scriptures "are able to make you wise for salvation through faith in Christ Jesus" (2 Tim. 3:15). Paul continues, "All Scripture is God-breathed and is useful for teaching, rebuking, correcting and training in righteousness, so that the servant of God may be thoroughly equipped for every good work" (3:16–17). Scripture is uniquely useful for two vital purposes: for salvation and godly living (faith and practice). Scripture uniquely prepares us for being made right with God and living lives pleasing to him.

The gospel is revealed in the biblical story of redemption—*not* through the wordless revelation through creation. The Scriptures alone reveal the means by which a human who has rebelled against God can be made righteous (Rom. 1:16–17). Only by grace alone through faith alone as revealed in the Scriptures alone (*sola Scriptura*) can one be made wise for salvation (cf. Rom. 3:21–24).

---

66 Taking Your Seat

Two important things to understand about the Word to the World, the Word in the World, and the World of the Word are that they are all genuine manifestations of God's revelation and that they are all interrelated. As we discuss doctrinal, moral, or practical issues, we must consider everything God has revealed related to the issues. Because none of the three cords is "truer" or "purer" than the others, we need to seek to better understand each in light of the other. So, for example, as you read Scripture, always ask how God's self-revelation in creation, in history, in your own life, and in Jesus Christ helps to illuminate your understanding. As you ponder the universe, your own experiences, and current events, always ask how Scripture shines light on the matters and how the person and work of Christ helps in comprehending their significance.

CONCLUSION

We know God because of his threefold revelation: the Word to the World, the Word in the World, and the World of the Word. These three means of revelation are in perfect harmony. They complement each other. One is not "truer" than the others; each is Truth. One is not "clearer" than the others; each sufficiently reveals what it is intended to convey. If we neglect one or two of these cords, therefore, we will be neglecting the gracious self-revelation of God.

The three cords of God's communication compel us toward theology in community. No individual Christian, however gifted he or she may be in time, talent, and intelligence, could possibly explore alone all the depths of God's Word to the World, Word in the World, or World of the Word. Because of this, we do theology together: the Interpreter, the Theologian, the Virtuous, the Philosopher, the Scientist, the Artist, the Minister, and the Historian.

 Jerusalem Council

Though all participants shared their own perspectives, experiences, and insights, only one opinion prevailed at the Jerusalem Council—God's. In Acts 15:6 (NASB), we read, "The apostles and the elders came together to look into this matter" The issue was clearly doctrinal and practical: what must one do to be saved? But the goal was not to see who could drum up the most "votes" or who could muster the most moving arguments. The goal was to seek the truth of God's revelation concerning the matter (15:28).

In relying on divine revelation, the members of the council appealed to God's Word to the World—the teachings of Holy Scripture applicable to the matter (Acts 15:14–15). They also reckoned with the Word in the World—the person and saving work of Jesus Christ and the continued work of the Spirit through the ministry of the apostles (15:7–12). And they drew insights from the World of the Word—the unfolding of history and resulting cultural and practical realities with which they had to cope, all the while drawing on God-given reason to synthesize their insights and arguments (15:19–29).

CHAPTER 4

THE ROLE OF THE INTERPRETER

❗ Centerpiece

Providing vital guidance in biblical exegesis and biblical theology, the Interpreter maintains the standard of inspired Scripture as the inviolable norming norm of theological method.

C hristian thinkers have always asserted that the accurate reading of Scripture plays a unique and central role in theological method. Scripture is unique as verbal revelation of God. That is, it consists of words that are from God; they are God-breathed (2 Tim. 3:16; cf. 2 Pet. 1:21). The word that Paul uses, *theopneustos*, is one he coined. He didn't invent the concept of the God-breathed quality of Scripture, but he did create a word to describe what people of faith have believed about the words of Scripture since the days of Moses. Scripture is from God (*theos*) by means of the breath or Spirit (*pneuma*).

Although written by human authors in a variety of places over a long period of time, the words of Scripture are God's words as well as human words. The Scriptures include a variety of human, culturally constructed genres such as narrative, prophecy, wisdom, poetry, apocalyptic, epistolary, gospels, and historical. Therefore, faithful translations of the sense of Scripture are inviolable affirmations of God's revealed truth. And faithful translations of the original

58

Hebrew, Aramaic, and Greek words of the Bible as well as sound explanations of the meaning of Scripture require the faithful work of an Interpreter. The Interpreter brings to the Table expertise in original languages, exegesis, hermeneutics, and a wide range of biblical scholarship.

The Interpreter seeks to present a faithful reflection of the verbally inspired Word to the World. However, because of the inherent limitations involved in the process of interpretation (both translation and elucidation), all interpreters "see in a mirror dimly" (1 Cor. 13:12 NASB). Both our eyesight and our looking glasses distort or diminish full and perfect understanding of Scripture. As such, the Interpreter must admit that the fruit of hard-won translations and understandings are really only a good faith reflection on the verbally inspired Word to the World. Whereas the words of God are unfailing, the words of the Interpreter are not.

As we discussed in chapter 2, "Revelation at the Center," theologians must always maintain a strict distinction between what the Bible *says* and what the Interpreter *says* the Bible says—or what the interpreting community says *about* what the Bible says. Further, the Interpreter is situated in a particular place and time, with certain experiences and perspectives, biases and prejudices—many of which she is unaware. In short, the Interpreter is finite—always and necessarily. Thus, the interpretation will always be finite, incomplete, and at points inaccurate. Yet Scripture must still be translated, read, studied, and interpreted. The role of the Interpreter is therefore a high and holy—as well as a sober and serious—calling.

THE CENTRAL ROLE OF SCRIPTURE IN THEOLOGICAL METHOD

Scripture plays a central role in theological method for two main reasons. First, because of its nature as verbal revelation—the Word to the World—it comes to us in a form that allows for almost immediate incorporation into theological dialogue. Theology as "discourse concerning God, his works, and his ways" necessarily requires us to work with ideas and concepts expressed in words—propositional truth claims. The Bible includes many propositional claims, defined as assertions which could be validated as true or false.[1] Because of what Christians believe about the nature of Scripture as inspired, we believe that Scripture is true in all it affirms. For example, "God is love" (1 John 4:8) is a proposition about God that is true. The Bible also contains non-propositional content: verbal revelation that does not make a claim but "also contains questions, injunctions, and wishes."[2] What makes the Bible central to theological method is that it is, in its entirety, the very words of God given by means of the Spirit. The Bible is reliable, inspired, verbal revelation. Thus, it rightly plays a central role in theological method.

But affirming that Scripture is God's very Word to the World doesn't remove the need for translation and interpretation. It's important to reiterate that all of our translations and interpretations of the original languages of the Bible are subject to correction. Thus, while what Scripture says in its original languages is a first-tier source of theology, what translators and interpreters say Scripture says is a second-tier source. Yet we should not regard faithful translations of the Bible as any less central to our theological method.[3] We should recall that many passages of Scripture are fairly easy to translate and pose no serious interpretational problems. Some passages, however, are "hard to understand" (2 Pet. 3:16). Because of the central role of Scripture as verbal revelation, the Interpreter must always enter theological discourse with humility, diligence, and a willingness to be corrected.

A second reason Scripture plays a unique and central role in theological method is its content. We imagine there are countless books that relay true information about a host of subjects from fields like science or history. Yet the Bible alone relays truths that answer questions most pertinent for theology: Where did we come from? Who is God,

---

1. See "Proposition, propositionalism," in *Pocket Dictionary of Theological Terms*, ed. Stanley J. Grenz, David Guretski, and Cherith Fee Nordling (Downers Grove: IVP, 1999), 96–97.

2. Daniel Hill, "Proposition," in *Dictionary for Theological Interpretation of the Bible*, ed. Kevin J. Vanhoozer (Grand Rapids: Baker Academic, 2005), 633. Hill continues, "The literary *genre* not only determines what proposition is affirmed—for example in irony the proposition affirmed is the opposite of the one that the sentence expresses—but also what it is that affirms the proposition, whether an individual sentence or a larger passage."

3. The sacred writings that Timothy's mother and grandmother taught him were translations (2 Tim. 3:15–16).

what is he like, and how do we know him? What is our purpose as humans? Why is there so much suffering, evil, and death? What's the answer to humanity's problems? Scripture plays a unique, central, and superior role in theological method because the content and purpose of its statements more directly answer the big questions and inform the major issues of theology. Only in Scripture is the gospel revealed, that Christ died "for our sins" (1 Cor. 15:3) and his resurrection is the basis of our hope (1 Cor. 15:17).

Because of its central role in theological method, we must address some vital truths about Scripture every Interpreter must always keep in mind.

❓ FAQ

If All Interpretation is Fallible, Can We Be Sure of Anything?

Yes, by God's gift of faith. Christian theology is "faith seeking understanding." Faith is, historically in Christian thought, a sufficient ground for knowledge. Faith provides confidence and even certainty that some things can be known. Our certainty is not driven by an objective analysis of evidence that leads to certainty, but by the Spirit of God who convicts, convinces, and compels people of the basic truths of the Christian faith (John 16:8, 13). Thus, even when we approach God's revelation, we come with a basic orientation of trusting its truthfulness (subjective faith) and a settled belief in the truthfulness of the fundamental doctrines of the faith (objective faith)—both by the Spirit. This will be further developed in chapter 5, "The Task of the Theologian."

SCRIPTURE DOESN'T CONTRADICT ITSELF

Scripture is true in everything it affirms.[4] This means that, properly interpreted, apparent conflicts or contradictions between two biblical assertions are just that—apparent. If one reads Passage 1 as teaching X and Passage 2 as teaching non-X, it's not the fault of the Scripture,

---

4. The common claim, "Every word in Scripture is true," fails to understand that the usage of the words is necessary to evaluate truth or error and, since Scripture includes false statements and lies by fools, humans, and the father of lies, inerrancy applies only to what Scripture affirms.

but the fault of the Interpreter. The Interpreter has either misread or misinterpreted Passage 1, Passage 2, or both!

This view of the non-contradiction of Scripture is ancient and enduring. For example, Irenaeus of Lyons (c. 180) challenged heretics who attempted to twist Scripture by breaking this fundamental rule of non-contradiction. He wrote,

> In all these passages, therefore, as I have already said, these men must either allege that the apostle expresses opinions contradicting himself . . . or, on the other hand, they will be forced to make perverse and crooked interpretations of all the passages, so as to overturn and alter the sense of the words. . . . And thus shall they be compelled to put a false interpretation upon passages such as these, they who do not choose to understand one correctly.[5]

However, this doesn't mean that we'll always be able to arrive at the correct interpretation of every passage subject to our investigation.[6] Nor does it mean that we have necessarily arrived at the proper interpretations simply because we haven't created any contradictions between passages. Humility is needed in every step of the interpretive process.

One reasonable implication of the non-contradictory nature of biblical affirmations is that clear passages should be used to help interpret passages that may be obscure in meaning. Again, Irenaeus helps here: "All Scripture, which has been given to us by God, shall be found by us perfectly consistent; and the parables shall harmonize with those passages which are perfectly plain; and those statements the meaning

---

5. See Irenaeus, *Against Heresies* 5.13.5 (ANF 1:541). Most of our patristic quotations will come from the *Ante-Nicene Fathers* (ANF) or the *Nicene and Post-Nicene Fathers* (NPNF); the parenthetical citation after the citation points to these sources. For example, "(ANF 3:34)" refers to volume 3, page 34 of the Roberts and Donaldson edition of *The Ante-Nicene Fathers*. The NPNF span two separate series, so for these we indicate the series in the first number (1 or 2), then the volume within that series, followed by the page within that volume. For example, "(NPNF 1.3:34)" refers to the first series of the *Nicene and Post-Nicene Fathers*, volume 3, page 34. Though there are more contemporary translations for some of these writings, we've chosen to use the ANF and NPNF because they are in the public domain and are easily accessible online at www.ccel.org.

6. Paul Helm, *The Providence of God* (Downers Grove: InterVarsity Press, 1994), 28, writes: "It is an axiom of the Christian faith that Scripture is self-consistent. And so it follows that *prima facie* contradictions or inconsistencies in the data must be capable of resolution."

of which is clear, shall serve to explain the parables; and through the many diversified utterances [of Scripture] there shall be heard one harmonious melody."[7]

WE MUST USE THE BIBLE THE WAY IT WAS MEANT TO BE USED

Scripture itself sets forth the Bible's intended uses. Scripture points us to Jesus Christ (Luke 24:27; John 5:39; Acts 8:35; 18:28; Rom. 1:2; 1 Cor. 15:3–4). It's to be read publically in church for instruction (1 Tim. 4:13). It also contains the wisdom of God needed to be saved and to walk in righteousness (Ps. 119:105; 2 Tim. 3:16–17). Rightly does the Church of England's "Thirty-nine Articles of Religion" summarize: "Holy Scripture containeth all things necessary to salvation: so that whatsoever is not read therein, nor may be proved thereby, is not to be required of any man, that it should be believed as an article of the faith, or be thought requisite or necessary to salvation."[8] In other words, the primary purpose of Scripture is to transform our thoughts and actions. It is sufficient for faith and practice.[9]

This does *not* mean that Scripture doesn't touch upon historical matters, philosophical issues, or scientific questions. It does address such things, and when it does, it does so truthfully. However, Scripture was not given to be a history textbook, a philosophical treatise, or a handbook of scientific facts. For that matter, the Bible isn't a guide for dieting, a leadership and management manual, a guide for "biblical economics," a pocketbook for political action, or a collection of frameworthy quotes to hang in your office. If the Bible was meant to point us to Jesus and equip believers for good works, we conscript it into illegitimate service when we use it to justify political opinions, glean dietary advice, or formulate scientific theories. Going to the Bible with

7. Irenaeus, *Against Heresies* 2.28.3 (ANF 1:400).

8. Article VI, "Of the Sufficiency of the Holy Scripture for Salvation," *Book of Common Prayer* (1801), accessed 14 February 2018, http://justus.anglican.org/resources/bcp/1928/Articles.htm.

9. Wayne Grudem explains it this way: "The sufficiency of Scripture means that Scripture contained all the words of God he intended his people to have at each stage of redemptive history, and that it now contains all the words of God we need for salvation, for trusting him perfectly, and for obeying him perfectly" (*Systematic Theology: An Introduction to Biblical Doctrine* [Grand Rapids: Zondervan, 1994], 127).

questions is appropriate; demanding that the Bible answer all of our questions—especially questions that arise in the modern world—is not appropriate. But when Scripture does speak, it speaks authoritatively.

Using the Bible the way it was meant to be used involves both asking questions Scripture actually answers and being satisfied with its sometimes (let's admit it) unsatisfying answers. When we ask the Bible questions it doesn't answer, we run into trouble. Irenaeus of Lyons puts it this way: "If, for instance, anyone asks, 'What was God doing before He made the world?' we reply that the answer to such a question lies with God Himself. For that this world was formed perfect by God, receiving a beginning in time, the Scriptures teach us; but no Scripture reveals to us what God was employed about before this event."[10]

We must use the Bible the way it was meant to be used. The Bible is the best-selling book of all time, widely read and studied, and the source of great comfort to some and consternation to others. The way we use the Bible matters. The Bible tells the great, *true* story of redemption, of a God who created a good world, watched as that world was corrupted by sin and rebellion, and is at work redeeming it on the trajectory to a new heaven and a new earth. The Bible is not a set of rules, a love letter, a book of magic words, or a science or history textbook.[11]

WE MUST READ THE BIBLE THE WAY IT WAS MEANT TO BE READ

The healthy emphasis on *personal* Bible study has sometimes led to a perspective that any individual believer with an open Bible and the Holy Spirit can employ an easy method and come out with the right biblical doctrine or practice. Sometimes the only method a Christian learns—even through Bible college or seminary training—is a variation of "observation," interpretation," and "application," or some other linear inductive Bible study method. This is an extremely helpful place to start.[12] But a more nuanced reading of the Bible recognizes that

---

10. Irenaeus, *Against Heresies* 2.28.3 (ANF 1:400).

11. See Glenn R. Kreider, "What Is the Bible?" *Fathom*, 10 October 2016, accessed 26 October 2017, https://www.fathommag.com/stories/what-is-the-bible.

12. We were taught this method to great benefit by Prof. Hendricks. See Howard G. Hendricks and William D. Hendricks, *Living by the Book: The Art and Science of Reading the Bible* (rev. ed., Chicago: Moody, 2007).

our observations are rooted in the experiences and knowledge of the observer; that interpretation is a human task and based upon the Interpreter's lens; and that we make applications in a world far removed in time and space from the world of the biblical text. But most problematic is that an individual method of personal Bible study often lacks emphasis on the importance of the community indwelled by the Spirit, of listening to the voices of others—both past and present— indwelled by the Spirit, and of having each Interpreter's interpretation tested by others by the power of the Spirit.

Our students often understand the doctrine of the clarity (or "perspicuity") of Scripture to mean that anyone can pick up, read, and understand the Bible rightly. These are graduate school students, many of whom are taking Greek and Hebrew language courses.[13] However, a proper Christian view of perspicuity is defined this way: "All things in Scripture are not alike plain in themselves, nor alike clear unto all: yet those things which are necessary to be known, believed, and observed for salvation are so clearly propounded, and opened in some place of Scripture or other, that not only the learned, but the unlearned, in a due use of the ordinary means, may attain unto a sufficient understanding of them."[14]

What are the "ordinary means" by which we are to read Scripture to understand its meaning? Haroutunian notes:

> Reformers, like Luther, Bucer, and Zwingli, as well as Calvin . . . agreed that the *natural* meaning of a statement was to be preferred to one arrived at by way of allegorizing or supplying a meaning other than the *literal*. This method was commonplace among humanists, who applied it to Greek and Roman writings earlier than to the Bible. Allegory was contrary to the humanistic canon

---

13. Burk Parsons, "The Perspicuity of Scripture," accessed 21 December 2017, https://www.ligonier.org/learn/articles/perspicuity-scripture/, summarizes our experience well: "Oddly enough, the word *perspicuity* is one of the more unclear words we could use to speak of clarity. What's more, when we say we believe in the perspicuity of Scripture, people sometimes get the wrong impression that we are implying that everything in Scripture is entirely clear and easy to understand. But that's not the case. We know this both from experience and because the Word of God itself tells us that not everything in it is easy to understand."

14. "Of the Holy Scripture," *Westminster Confession of Faith*, accessed 20 December 2017, http://www.reformed.org/documents/wcf_with_proofs/.

of interpretation; and "literalism," that is, the desire to get at an author's own mind, was of its essence.[15]

However, a caution must be recognized: "Neither the humanists nor Calvin meant by the literal meaning necessarily an unspiritual meaning. The natural interpretation of a passage for them was one that did justice to the *intention* of the author. When Calvin protested against allegorizing, he was protesting not against finding a spiritual meaning in a passage, but against finding one that was not there."[16] Along with the vast majority of orthodox interpreters of Scripture from the first century onward, the Reformers pursued a Christ-centered spiritual significance to the natural, literal meaning of Scripture—one that was intended by the divine author, not imported by the reader.[17]

In classic Christian theology, a proper understanding of the inspiration of Scripture leads to a number of methodical "rules of thumb" for reading, interpreting, and applying God's Word to the World.[18] These include:

- The words of Scripture are God-breathed, so they are incapable of error in what they affirm. They cannot be corrected by any other written authority.
- The words of Scripture are also written through humans, so they follow the normal "rules" of grammar, syntax, and genre. They communicate to humans in human language.

---

15. Joseph Haroutunian, "General Introduction," in *Calvin: Commentaries*, ed. and trans. Joseph Haroutunian and Louise Pettibone Smith, The Library of Christian Classics, Ichthus ed., ed. John Baillie, John T. McNeill, and Henry P. Van Dusen (Philadelphia: Westminster, 1958), 28.

16. Haroutunian, "General Introduction," 28.

17. See Richard A. Muller, "Biblical Interpretation in the Era of the Reformation: The View from the Middle Ages," in *Biblical Interpretation in the Era of the Reformation: Essays Presented to David C. Steinmetz in Honor of His Sixtieth Birthday*, ed. Richard A. Muller and John L. Thompson (Grand Rapids: Eerdmans, 1996), 3–22.

18. Christian college and seminary courses in inductive methodical Bible study methods, biblical interpretation, and exegesis will provide a much fuller account of the methods involved in biblical hermeneutics. It is not our intention to preview or review the vital content of those courses of study. The purpose here is to place the results of exegetical methods in the context of the larger method of theological discourse.

- The big picture within which the parts of Scripture are to be understood is the Trinitarian creation-fall-redemption narrative centered on the person and work of Christ in his first and second coming—what the early church called the "Rule of Faith" (see discussion in chapters 5 and 11).
- The Holy Spirit is both the one who inspired Scripture as its divine author as well as the one who holds the key to proper interpretation and application.
- The individual's reading needs to be tested in the community of the Spirit. Scripture was never meant to be read apart from a context of discipleship and accountability.
- Context is vitally important in determining the meaning of a text—words are only understood in the contexts of their sentences, sentences in their paragraphs, paragraphs in books, books in testaments, and testaments in the canon of Scripture.
- The Old Testament is the most immediate background for understanding the New Testament, though truths about God more clearly revealed in the New Testament were just as true in the Old.
- Just as we must understand the historical, cultural, geographic, chronological, and theological context of the time and place of the Scriptures, we must also recognize our own unique context and perspectives as we ask and answer contemporary questions of the ancient text.
- The goal of biblical interpretation is application—life change—producing lives of virtue: faith, love, and hope. It is not merely an academic pursuit for the sake of knowledge.

At the Table

The persona of the Interpreter represents a variety of fields related directly and indirectly to the study of the Old and New Testsaments. This includes study of the original languages in which the Bible was written—Hebrew, Aramaic, and Greek—as well as Bible translation. It also encompasses foundational disciplines like textual criticism (the study of ancient manuscripts for the purpose of confirming the original text of Scripture), bible backgrounds (exploring the history, archaeology, and culture of the world in which the Bible was originally written and read), and hermeneutics (the principles involved in establishing the proper meaning of a text). Thus, the Interpreter necessarily depends on others at the Table—the Scientist (archaeology), the Historian (backgrounds), and the Philosopher (hermeneutics). The Interpreter also represents the broad fields of Old and New Testament studies, biblical theology (studying biblical themes of particular books, authors, testaments, or in the entire canon), and Bible exposition (presenting the interpretation of Scripture in a way that brings out the meaning of the text for the purpose of transformation). These activities intersect with the Theologian (biblical theology), the Minister (exposition), the Virtuous (transformation), and the Artist (communication).

SCRIPTURE WAS NEVER MEANT TO BE THE ONLY SOURCE FOR THEOLOGY

Some reading this may take a cursory glance at our discussion of sources (plural!) of theology and accuse us of betraying the Protestant rallying cry, "SOLA SCRIPTURA!"—Latin for "Scripture alone!" So much misinformation about *sola Scriptura* is floating around in Christian circles. Many believe it means that the Bible—and the Bible *alone*—is the only source of truth for theological reflection and formulation. However, this is simply not true.[19]

Rather, *sola Scriptura* means that Scripture alone is the only inerrant source of verbally inspired truth available to the church today. It is the *norma normans non normata*—the "norming norm which cannot be normed." This means that if Scripture affirms one thing, but a Pope or a popular preacher affirms something different, Scripture *alone* is the final authority in the matter. Or if God's written Word to the

---

19. For some helpful discussions, see John R. Franke, "Scripture, Tradition, and Authority: Reconstructing the Evangelical Conception of *Sola Scriptura*," in *Evangelicals and Scripture: Tradition, Authority, and Hermeneutics,* ed. Vincent Bacote, Laura C. Miguélez, and Dennis L. Okholm (Downers Grove: InterVarsity, 2004), 192–201; Timothy George, *Theology of the Reformers* (Nashville: Broadman & Holman, 1988; revised ed., 2013), 384–87; Keith A. Mathison, *The Shape of Sola Scriptura* (Moscow, ID: Canon Press, 2011), 19–156.

World contradicts a truth-claim from science, philosophy, experience, or even a church council, creed, or confession, all those truth-claims must bow to the authority of God's Word. No other source of verbal truth-claims can be used to correct the affirmations of Scripture, and no other authority—Pope, council, or popular consensus—occupies a seat of higher authority in the church than Scripture.

Theologian Mary Veeneman rightly observes: "Although it was not Luther's intention, some have interpreted the *sola scriptura* principle to insist that the biblical text must be the only source of theology and that no other sources have any bearing on that work."[20] Veeneman notes two problems with this false definition of *sola Scriptura*. First, "Luther did not intend the *sola scriptura* principle to suggest that scripture should be the only source of theology. His understanding of *sola scriptura* was that scripture is to be the chief source of theology."[21]

Second, "despite claims about the Bible being self-interpreting, it seems that there often isn't an immediately apparent plain reading of the text."[22] This means that other sources or resources for theological method must help us to interpret the Bible properly. And the Bible helps us interpret those other sources, too. God's Word helps us interpret God's World . . . and God's World helps us interpret God's Word. At the same time, the Word who came into the World, Jesus Christ, is the interpretive lens and the hermeneutical goal of both the Word and the World.

This clarification of *sola Scriptura* is important as we move around the Table and explore various fields of inquiry—from the task of the Theologian to the quest of the Philosopher, from the pursuit of the Scientist to the labor of the Minister. Each of these offers wisdom, insight, and truth drawn from the wells of God's threefold revelation. If we begin theological method with an unbiblical understanding of *sola Scriptura*, then we will never be able to learn proper "table manners."

---

20. Mary M. Veeneman, *Introducing Theological Method: A Survey of Contemporary Theologians and Approaches* (Grand Rapids: Baker Academic, 2017), 11.

21. Veeneman, *Introducing Theological Method*, 11–12. See also Henk van den Belt, "Sola Scriptura: An Inadequate Slogan for the Authority of Scripture," *Calvin Theological Journal* 51 (2016): 204–26.

22. Veeneman, *Introducing Theological Method*, 12.

66 Taking Your Seat

The Interpreter is one of the seats at the Table that every believer occupies to some degree. Because of the central place of Scripture as God's only inspired written revelation, every participant in the theological discourse must reckon with the text of Scripture. You can't set aside Scripture and just practice philosophical theology, practical theology, or natural theology. Though questions and issues may generate from other places at the Table, and those places may contribute significantly to our understanding of Scripture, the interpretation of Scripture is most likely the starting point and center point of our discourse concerning God, his works, and his ways. Therefore, you can't afford to be a sloppy Interpreter. You may never learn Hebrew, Aramaic, or Greek, but you need to become thoroughly familiar with the contents of the Bible by reading it repeatedly. And you need to learn basic principles of healthy interpretation. Ask your pastor, teacher, mentor, or professor for recommendations. Remember, we don't interpret Scripture in a vacuum, but we are all interpreting Scripture.

CONCLUSION

The Interpreter provides vital guidance through careful biblical exegesis—reading Scripture in the original Hebrew, Aramaic, and Greek languages, providing modern-language translations and commentary, and moving us toward an understanding of the meaning and intention of the inspired Word of God. Biblical theology is a development of the thoughts and themes of the Bible's own teachings concerning God, his works, and his ways. And because of the unique focus and purpose of God's revelation through the Word to the World, the role of the Interpreter is paramount.

However, biblical interpretation is the beginning—not the end—of theological method. As the only verbally inspired truth available to us today, Scripture serves as the cornerstone of theological method. But Scripture itself points outside itself to other means by which God has made himself known. Though we should never let go of a firm grip on Scripture and thus never belittle the role of the Interpreter, we should also seek to better understand what God is saying to us through his

Word to the World by attending diligently to the Word in the World and the World of the Word.

Jerusalem Council

When Judaizers added circumcision to the gospel and demanded the Gentiles to obey the Law of Moses (Acts 15:1, 5), they no doubt had passages from the Old Testament to support their position (e.g., Exod. 12:48). The question was not which side was using Scripture but which side was reading and applying Scripture rightly.

With Bible in hand, James chimed in, adding an important insight into the plan God had for the salvation of the Gentiles from the beginning. In response to the report from Peter that Gentiles had received the Holy Spirit by faith apart from any works of the Law (Acts 15:8–9), James said, "The words of the prophets are in agreement with this, as it is written: 'After this I will return and rebuild David's fallen tent. Its ruins I will rebuild, and I will restore it, that the rest of mankind may seek the Lord, even all the Gentiles who bear my name, says the Lord, who does these things'—things known from long ago" (Acts 15:15–18). In this instance, James took on *the role of the Interpreter* in reading and applying Scripture to the matter at hand (15:19).

CHAPTER 5

THE TASK OF THE THEOLOGIAN

Centerpiece

Guided by the "Rule of Faith" as a confessional cornerstone, the Theologian helps guide the conversation through attention to the center, the story, and the standards of the Great Tradition believed, taught, and confessed in the body of Christ worldwide.

It has become common in some Christian circles to say, "Everybody's a theologian." One writer puts it this way: "All Christians are theologians, but some are more able theologians than others."[1] On one hand, if we broadly define theology as "thinking about God" or "talking about God," then everybody who might think or talk about God is, in this general sense, a "theologian."[2] On the other hand, suggesting that anybody who thinks or talks about God is a theologian is a little like saying anyone who thinks or talks about his health is a physician. Not quite. We can treat a wound without being a surgeon, cook meals without being a chef, or talk about God without being a theologian.

On the *other* other hand, it's true that we all *do* theology in the sense of carrying on discourse concerning God, his works, and his ways.

---

1. Graeme Goldsworthy, *According to Plan: The Unfolding Revelation of God in the Bible* (Downers Grove, IL: InterVarsity Press, 2002), 29.

2. See, for example, Stanley J. Grenz and Roger E. Olson, *Who Needs Theology?: An Invitation to the Study of God* (Downers Grove, IL: InterVarsity Press, 1996), 12–13.

And we all think and live in light of our theology—whether consciously or unconsciously, whether Christians, theists, atheists, or agnostics.[3] Yet some people have special training and experience in a systematic, methodical, and intentional pursuit of Christian theology. Technically speaking, those people are properly called "theologians."

But what is the actual task of the Theologian? Simply put, the task of the Theologian, under the broad pursuit of "faith seeking understanding," is always to ask and strive to answer the question, "How does this fit?" That is, how do the various truths concerning God, his works, and his ways—from any and every source—relate to each other and to the Christian faith? The Theologian's task is one of *synthesis*.[4]

In this work of synthesis, and guided by the God-revealed pattern of the Christian faith, the Theologian builds on doctrinal standards believed, taught, and confessed in the body of Christ worldwide and throughout history. The Theologian helps his or her fellow Christians at the Table to think through how their various contributions fit into "the faith that was once for all entrusted" to God's people (Jude 3).

"THE FAITH" AS THE CENTER, THE STORY, AND THE STANDARDS

A classic description of the task of theology is *fides quaerens intellectum*, often translated as "faith seeking understanding." However, this Latin phrase is cloaked in a double entendre. Latin has no article. The noun *fide*, like its Greek equivalent, *pistis*, can mean subjective belief, as in Ephesians 2:8 ("by grace you have been saved, through faith"). The term can also mean the objective content of the faith as in Jude 3

---

3. One of our teachers, Charles Ryrie, wrote, "Everyone *is* a theologian—of one sort or another. . . . Theology simply means thinking about God and expressing those thoughts in some way . . . Even an atheist has a theology. He thinks about God, rejects His existence, and expresses that sometimes in creed and always in lifestyle" (Charles Ryrie, *Basic Theology* [Wheaton: Victor Books, 1986; reprint, Chicago: Moody Publishers, 1999], 9).

4. The nineteenth-century Princeton theologian Charles Hodge noted that we "must endeavor to bring all the facts of revelation into systematic order and mutual relation" in order to "exhibit their truth, vindicate them from objections, or bring them to bear in their full force on the minds of men" (Charles Hodge, *Systematic Theology*, vol. 1 [New York: Scribner, 1871; Reprint, Grand Rapids: Eerdmans, 1940], 2–3).

("contend for the faith"). If the task of the Theologian is *fides quaerens intellectum,* is it seeking understanding by means of a believing and trusting disposition? Or is it seeking understanding within the community of faith by building on the content of the faith?

We believe both elements are essential to the task of the Theologian. Building on the "givens" of the content of the Christian faith, the Theologian seeks to better understand this faith through a manner consistent with a believing and faithful disposition. The subjective definition of faith is not too complicated: it's knowing, believing, and trusting in something or someone. But what is the actual content of "the faith that was once for all entrusted to God's holy people" (Jude 3)? If this body of Christian truth is the incorruptible foundation, the immovable boundary, and the irreplaceable center point for theology, then *what exactly does this include?*

In the ancient church, "the faith" was summed up in what was called the "Rule of the Faith" (*regula fidei*) or the "Canon of the Truth" (*canona tēs alētheias*). The second-century pastor and teacher, Irenaeus of Lyons, received the fundamental truths of the faith from his own pastor and teacher, Polycarp of Smyrna, who himself had been a direct disciple of the apostle John. Around the year AD 180, Irenaeus summed up the basic content and contours of the faith this way:

> This, then, is the order of the rule of our faith, and the foundation of the building, and the stability of our conversation. God, the Father, not made, not material, invisible; one God, the Creator of all things: this is the first point of our faith. The second point is: the Word of God, Son of God, Christ Jesus our Lord, who was manifested to the prophets according to the form of their prophesying and according to the method of the dispensation of the Father: through whom all things were made; who also at the end of the times, to complete and gather up all things, was made man among men, visible and tangible, in order to abolish death and show forth life and produce a community of union between God and man. And the third point is: the Holy Spirit, through whom the prophets prophesied, and the fathers learned

the things of God, and the righteous were led forth into the way of righteousness; and who in the end of the times was poured out in a new way upon mankind in all the earth, renewing man unto God.[5]

❓ FAQ

What Is the Regula Fidei (Rule of Faith)?

The *Regula Fidei* (also known as the "Rule of Faith" or "Canon of the Truth" is a brief but comprehensive summary of the biblical narrative of creation-fall-redemption which starts with God the Father's creation of everything, continues with God the Son's incarnation, atoning death, resurrection, ascension, and anticipated return, and culminating in God the Spirit's work in forming, transforming, and moving God's people toward consummation in resurrection and restoration. The early church used the *Regula Fidei* as a starting point for instruction of new believers as well as a guide for reading Scripture in light of its own story and basic Christian doctrine. Later confessions and creeds were based on the content of the original *Regula Fidei*.

Others in the early church described the Rule of Faith in a variety of ways, all of them articulating the same basic truths.[6] Whether part of training for new believers, a baptismal confession, a creedal formula, or a treatise on theology, these various expressions of the faith all covered the same basic content. They relay the Trinitarian account of creation and redemption: all things are from the Father, through the Son, by the Spirit—creation, revelation, redemption, and ultimate restoration. They pay particular attention to the person and work of Christ—his deity and humanity, his saving death and resurrection, and his present and future work as high priest and king. And these summaries of the faith provide clear and concise means of communicating the essential storyline of God's revelation in Scripture, in Christ, and in creation. The basic content of the Rule of Faith should

---

5. Irenaeus, *Demonstration of the Apostolic Preaching* 7. In *St. Irenaeus: The Demonstration of the Apostolic Preaching*, trans. J. Armitage Robinson (London: SPCK, 1920), 74–75.

6. The oft-recited Apostles' Creed functions as a good early expression of this rule.

be the starting point for training new believers, for baptizing disciples, for composing doctrinal statements, and for determining genuineness of a Christian confession.

So, to define the faith briefly, we might put it this way: *The faith is the Trinitarian creation-fall-redemption narrative centered on the person and work of Christ in his first and second coming.* A great way to expand on this definition is to think of it in terms of the Center, the Story, and the Standards.[7]

The Center of Theology

At any point in history, we can find a variety of theological systems organized around differing centers.[8] John Miley noted, "Some regard one truth as the more central and determining, while in the view of others . . . some other truth should hold the ruling place. Such truth, whatever it may be, determines the method of systematization."[9] We can distinguish various theological systems by such distinct centers, or organizing principles. The following is just a sampling:

Theocentric: centered on God's nature and being, usually "divinity" in the abstract.[10]

Anthropocentric: centered on humanity's needs, experiences, and abilities.[11]

---

7. This is a modified and adapted version of a similar definition of "orthodoxy" found in one of the authors' books, which summarizes the orthodox faith with the Center, the Story, and the Markers. See Michael J. Svigel, *RetroChristianity: Reclaiming the Forgotten Faith* (Wheaton: Crossway, 2012), 87–97.

8. Stanley J. Grenz called this the "integrative motif," defined as "the central idea that provides the thematic perspective in light of which all other theological concepts are understood and given their relative meaning or value" (Stanley J. Grenz, *Theology for the Community of God*, 2d ed. [Grand Rapids: Eerdmans/Vancouver, B.C.: Regent College Publishing, 2000], 20–21).

9. John Miley, *Systematic Theology*, vol. 1, Library of Biblical and Theological Literature, ed. George R. Crooks and John F. Hurst, vol. 5 (New York: Hunt & Eaton, 1898), 51.

10. See, e.g., R.C. Sproul, *What Is Reformed Theology?: Understanding the Basics* (Grand Rapids: Baker, 1997), 20, 29.

11. We know of no theologian who would self-identify as "anthropocentric." This description

Bibliocentric: centered on God's propositional revelation in
   Scripture.[12]
Ecclesiocentric: centered on the redeemed community of the
   church and its mission.[13]
Eschatocentric: centered in the culmination of all things in the
   new creation.[14]
Christocentric: centered on the person and work of Jesus Christ.

With the great majority of Christian thinkers, especially the most ancient, we affirm a christocentric theology in which the person and work of Jesus Christ in his first and second coming is the gravitational center of God's revelation, of Scripture, of history, of reality, and therefore of theology. Nineteenth-century Methodist theologian William Burt Pope urged that Jesus Christ "is the centre of theology; all its doctrines revolve around Him."[15]

So, the faith centers on the person and work of Christ in his first and second coming. This is a Trinitarian narrative, since Jesus Christ is the second person of the Godhead, and his work cannot be disconnected from the perfect harmony of the Trinity. Jesus is the central theme of the Bible, theology, Christian life, and all reality. The Hebrew Scriptures look forward to his coming, the New Testament tells the story of his first coming and looks forward to the culmination of the plan of redemption in his second coming.[16]

---

is used by critics of seventeenth- to nineteenth-century liberal theologies that shifted from traditional confessional Christianity and its sources and authorities to a humanity-centered interest in religion. Charles Taylor describes four directions of change during the seventeenth and eighteenth centuries that "[reduce] the role and place of the transcendent" and contribute to a "striking anthropocentric shift" in theology (Charles Taylor, *A Secular Age* [Cambridge, MA: Harvard University Press, 2007], 222–24).

12. See Edward J. Carnell, *The Case for Orthodox Theology* (1959; reprint, Eugene, OR: Wipf & Stock, 2005), 33–35.

13. This has sometimes been the tendency of the Eastern Orthodox and Roman Catholic approaches. Cardinal Joseph Ratzinger (a.k.a. Pope Benedict XVI), is quoted as saying, "Theology either exists in the church and from the church, or it does not exist at all," referring, of course, to the Roman Catholic Church (quoted in John L. Allen, Jr., *Pope Benedict XVI: A Biography of Joseph Ratzinger* [New York: Continuum, 2000], 31).

14. See Jürgen Moltmann, "Theology as Eschatology," in *The Future of Hope: Theology as Eschatology*, ed. Frederick Herzog (New York: Herder and Herder, 1970), 1–50.

15. William Burt Pope, *A Compendium of Christian Theology: Being Analytical Outlines of a Course of Theological Study, Biblical, Dogmatic, Historical*, vol. 1 (London: Beveridge, 1879), 10.

16. For a summary of this story of redemption, see Glenn R. Kreider, *God with Us: Exploring God's Personal Interactions with His People throughout the Bible* (Phillipsburg, NJ: P&R, 2014).

The eighteenth-century Puritan pastor-theologian Jonathan Edwards vividly summarized the centrality of Christ in God's plan of redemption this way:

1. That [from] the fall of man until the incarnation of Christ, God was doing those things that were preparatory to Christ's coming and working out redemption and which were forerunners and earnests of it.
2. That the time from Christ's incarnation until his resurrection was spent in procuring or purchasing redemption.
3. That the space of time from the resurrection of Christ until the end of the world is all taken up in bringing about or accomplishing the great effect or success of that purchase.[17]

As simple as it sounds, Christianity is about Christ. His person and work is the center of theology. The task of the Theologian is to preserve and promote the ordering of God's revelation around him.

The Story of Theology

Eugene Peterson asserts, "Story is the primary verbal means of bringing God's word to us. For that we can be most grateful, for story is our most accessible form of speech . . . The only serious rival to story in terms of accessibility and attraction is song, and there are plenty of those in the Bible too."[18] When we say that the faith is a story, we don't mean that the Bible weaves a tapestry of myths and legends intended merely to inspire readers with illustrations of virtue. Nor do we mean the accounts of people, places, and events are actually characters, settings, and scenes of a non-historical drama. God's true unfolding story

---

17. Jonathan Edwards, "Sermon Two" in *A History of the Work of Redemption*, ed. John F. Wilson and John E. Smith, vol. 9, The Works of Jonathan Edwards (New Haven; London: Yale University Press, 1989), 128.

18. Eugene H. Peterson, *Eat this Book: A Conversation in the Art of Spiritual Reading* (Grand Rapids: Eerdmans, 2006), 40. See also Russell Moore, "Have Bible Quoters Replaced Bible Readers?" Blog: *Russell Moore*, 16 January 2018, accessed 14 February 2018, https://www.russellmoore.com/2018/01/16/bible-quoters-replaced-bible-readers/, and "You Can't Have Ethics Without Stories," Blog, *Russell Moore*, 17 January 2018, https://www.russellmoore.com/2018/01/17/you-cant-have-ethics-without-stories/.

isn't *less* than history; it's *more* than history. The story of theology is the overarching biblical narrative of creation, fall and redemption, and ultimate restoration put into effect by the harmonious work of the triune God—*from* the Father, *through* the Son, and *by* the Holy Spirit.[19] In short, history really is *his* story, and his story is *our* story. Peterson explains, "Story doesn't just tell us something and leave it there, it invites our participation. A good story-teller gathers us into the story. We feel the emotions, get caught up in the drama, identify with the characters, see into nooks and crannies of life that we have overlooked, realize that there is more to this business of being human than we had yet explored."[20]

This story principally concerns the one true God—eternally existing as Father, Son, and Holy Spirit. From the moment that Jesus's disciples began pondering the deity of Christ as distinct from the Father and the reality of the divine presence through the person of the Holy Spirit, Christian theology has been bounded by—and bound to—reflection on the triune God. The eighteenth-century Anglican bishop and Oxford professor George Horne describes the faith as "that system of truths revealed in the holy Scriptures concerning the dispensations of the God whom we adore and into whose name we are baptized; the Father, the Son, and the Holy Spirit; three Persons in one God. These truths are proposed to us as the ground of our hope, our comfort, and our joy; as the principles on which the conduct of life is to be framed, accepted, and rewarded."[21]

The task of the Theologian does not *result* in the Trinitarian creation-fall-redemption story; it *begins* with the Trinitarian creation-fall-redemption story. The Trinitarian theology of the Christian

---

19. Though variously articulated, theologians tend to express "the story" of the Trinitarian creation-fall-redemption narrative in strikingly similar movements and terms, sometimes with two acts (creation-redemption), sometimes expanding it into three (creation-fall-redemption), and sometimes even four (creation-fall-redemption-restoration) or five (creation-fall-promise-redemption-restoration). See Sameer Yadav, "Christian Doctrine as Ontological Commitment to a Narrative," in *The Task of Dogmatics: Explorations in Theological Method,* ed. Oliver D. Crisp and Fred Sanders (Grand Rapids: Zondervan, 2017), 76.

20. Peterson, *Eat this Book*, 40–41.

21. George Horne, *The Duty of Contending for the Faith: A Sermon Preached at the Primary Visitation of the Most Reverend John, Lord Archbishop of Canterbury in the Cathedral and Metropolitical Church, on Saturday, July 1, 1786,* new ed. (London: Rivington, 1809), 4.

church is not to be demonstrated and proved to convince believers of its truth, but to persuade unbelievers of its veracity. And the task of theology is to expound upon how the triune God has been at work throughout the true story of creation and redemption. Whether center stage or backstage, every act in the drama of the creation and redemption of women and men is from the Father, through the Son, and by the Holy Spirit.

Having said that the story principally concerns the triune God, we must also say—not with a "but," but rather with an "also"—that the story principally concerns the person and work of Christ in his first and second coming. Prior to the coming of Christ, the narrative of creation, fall, and promise all pointed to Jesus Christ. His future coming and saving work were foreshadowed through types and images (Luke 24:25–27; 44–45; John 1:45; Acts 28:23; Heb. 10:1, 7) and foretold through prophecies (Matt. 26:56; Luke 18:31; Acts 3:18; Rom. 1:2–4; 1 Cor. 15:3–4). Through the miracle of his incarnation, Christ added to his fully divine person the full nature of humanity and thus eternally united to himself a permanent connection to this finite creation. By means of his atoning death and resurrection, Christ redeemed that fallen creation and transferred it to a new quality of existence—glory and immortality. And through the promise of his future return, Christ has sealed the certainty of the liberation and restoration of all creation.[22] The Holy Spirit is the deposit and guarantee (Eph. 1:13–14), the firstfruits (Rom. 8:23) of completion of that work of redemption. Thus, the Trinitarian creation-fall-redemption narrative pivots on the person and work of Christ in his first and second coming.

Both of these—the persons and works of the Trinity and the person and work of Christ—are essential, immovable elements of the story of theology—the gospel, or "good story"—of the faith.[23] Vanhoozer and Treier put it well:

---

22. "Restoration" is not merely a return to the original Edenic creation, but a new creation, a re-creation, an infinitely better creation than the original.

23. See Darren Sumner, "Christocentrism and the Immanent Trinity: Identifying Theology's Pattern and Norm," in *The Task of Dogmatics: Explorations in Theological Method*, ed. Oliver D. Crisp and Fred Sanders (Grand Rapids: Zondervan, 2017), 155–60.

Though many aspects of the gospel deserve attention and adoration, at its heart is the message that because of God the incarnate Son's cross and resurrection, people from every tribe and nation can have a filial fellowship with God the Father through God the Holy Spirit. Mere evangelical theology is thus *Trinity-centric* and *crucicentric*. At the center of both these centers stands the person of Jesus Christ.[24]

At the Table

The figure of the Theologian embodies a wide variety of disciplines. As a highly interdisciplinary pursuit, the multifaceted field of theology overlaps with a number of others at the Table. It has a hand in biblical theology (studying biblical themes of particular books, authors, testaments, or of the entire canon). It includes historical theology and the history of doctrine (studying continuities, discontinuities, developments, and deviations throughout the church's history), philosophical theology (using philosophical methods, theories, and concepts for asking and answering theological questions), and practical theology (reflection on personal, pastoral, social, moral, and ecclesiastical matters of practical concern). The Theologian also includes the more focused disciplines of confessional or dogmatic theology (theology authoritatively held and taught by particular denominations or church traditions) and systematic theology (understanding, organizing, and articulating truth about God, his works, and his ways in light of all of all means of God's revelation and all sources for theological reflection). Thus, the task of the Theologian frequently intersects with the work of the Interpreter, the Historian, the Philosopher, the Scientist, the Minister, the Virtuous, and the Artist.

The Standards of Theology

The essential doctrinal content of the Trinitarian creation-fall-redemption narrative centered on the person and work of Christ in his first and second coming has always been summarized by "classic ordinances," "church confessions," "universal creeds," and "doctrinal

---

24. Kevin J. Vanhoozer and Daniel J. Treier, *Theology and the Mirror of Scripture: A Mere Evangelical Account,* Studies in Christian Doctrine and Scripture (Downers Grove: InterVarsity, 2015), 79.

statements." These standards of sound theology, framing what has been called the "Great Tradition" of the classic orthodox Christian faith, have always been the guides for teaching new believers and as criteria for holding the faithful to a trustworthy belief and practice. The task of the Theologian—and for all participants at the Table—is to utilize such standards to aid in the church's doctrinal identity as "the pillar and foundation of the truth" (1 Tim. 3:15). Scripture must be read and applied, creation perceived and enjoyed, and Christ known and loved in the illuminating rays of the "Great Tradition"—the standards of theology.

Rightly practiced, the *classic ordinances* of baptism and the Lord's Supper repeatedly point believers back to the center of the story—the person and work of Jesus Christ. Those who are baptized are united with Christ in his death, burial, and resurrection. This reflects the work of the Holy Spirit, who unites believers to the body of Christ and initiates them into a relationship of adoption as children of God the Father. Through baptism, believers become part of the creation-fall-redemption narrative themselves. Then, the Lord's Supper (or "Communion," "Eucharist," or "Lord's Table") continually confesses the incarnation of the Word with true body and blood, uniting the body of Christ in consecration, and proclaiming the Lord's death until the risen Savior comes again.

From the beginning of the church's mission to make disciples, *church confessions* played a vital role in a person's initiation. Christians were baptized "in the name of the Father and of the Son and of the Holy Spirit" (Matt. 28:19). Early on, this initiation to discipleship was accompanied by a profession of faith in the events of creation-fall-redemption associated with the three persons. These confessions, which often varied in specific language from church to church, served as baptismal professions, as candidates for baptism or their sponsors recited or responded to a threefold Trinitarian statement that began with "I believe" (*credo*). To quote George Horne, "The different articles of our belief, dispersed in the Scriptures, were very early collected in summaries, styled Creeds, recited at baptism, and constituting thenceforth the badge and test of a man's profession."[25]

---

25. Horne, *The Duty of Contending for the Faith*, 4–5.

In the fourth and fifth centuries, major challenges to classic ortho-dox theology caused the far-flung churches throughout the world to draw their diverse confessions together to form *universal creeds*. These creeds and their definitions—forged through the controversy and conflicts at the first four universal church councils—Nicaea (325), Constantinople (381), Ephesus (431), and Chalcedon (451)—would serve as standards of proper belief concerning the triune God and the person of Jesus Christ. The creeds of Nicaea and Constantinople, as well as the Definition of Chalcedon, have stood the test of time. Even today, they stand as permanent monuments of the living faith. D. H. Williams notes, "Like guideposts along a precipitous mountain pass, the consensual creeds and theological writings of patristic Christi-anity were meant to mark the path of doctrinal trustworthiness and theological constancy, as they still do, for every subsequent generation of pilgrims."[26]

Finally, and much more recently, *doctrinal statements* serve to rearticulate in summary fashion the essential truths of the faith in clear, concise language. Good doctrinal statements not only cover all of the major doctrines of the Christian faith but also remind Chris-tians of the teachings and practices that are fundamental while dis-tinguishing these from others that are less foundational to Christian identity and unity. The Christian faith has, as it were, load-bearing doctrines, the removal of which would cause the entire superstructure of the faith itself to fail. It also has less fundamental articles of belief that may differ from believer to believer or from church to church. For doctrinal statements to serve as beneficial standards for the fruitful flourishing of Christian theology, they must focus on the fundamen-tals of the faith—not on distinctive doctrines and practices of individ-uals or denominations, nor on detailed interpretations of passages for which there has never been a unanimous consensus.

Creeds summarize the "once for all entrusted to God's holy people" (Jude 3), that is, essential, foundational doctrines of Christi-anity. Confessions of faith are a contextualization of that faith in a

---

26. D. H. Williams, *Retrieving the Tradition and Renewing Evangelicalism: A Primer for Suspicious Protestants* (Grand Rapids: Eerdmans, 1999), 172.

particular place or time. Such confessions, or doctrinal statements, distinguish one community's belief and practice from others. Baptists, Presbyterians, and Methodists each affirm Christian orthodoxy as expressed in the ecumenical creeds but they practice the faith differently, as expressed in their confessions.[27]

Together, these standards should not be viewed as a hindrance to a detailed study of Scripture, a deeper understanding of the faith, or a greater progress in doctrinal refinement. Rather, the standards function like maps, signposts, and compasses to aid us on our journey in the task of theology.

66 Taking Your Seat

You're already a Theologian, in a sense. You've thought about and talked about God, his works, and his ways. But you can be a better one. In a sense, anybody sitting at the Table and contributing to the discourse from any angle is participating in theology. But the more narrowly-focused contribution of the Theologian might be what we call "systematic theology." In your own emphasis—whether that's biblical exegesis, practical Christian living, worship, historical scholarship, missions, or something else—never lose sight of the center, the story, and the standards. Giving attention to these will keep you from becoming idiosyncratic, divisive, and schismatic. You'll be able to maintain an emphasis on the main things of the faith. And you'll discover that the list of opinions you're willing to fight over with other believers gets shorter as you unify around the core matters of orthodoxy and orthopraxy—right doctrine and right living.

CONCLUSION

Though all men and women at the Table are engaging in theological reflection and dialogue, the trained *Theologian* offers insight into the necessary task of synthesis. Ever before the Theologian is the question, "How does this fit?"

---

27. For a discussion of the relationship between creeds and confessions, see "The Language of Theology," *The Table Podcast*, 23 August 2016, accessed 20 February 2018, https://voice.dts .edu/tablepodcast/language-theology/.

If the Historian uncovers ancient sources on the conflict between orthodoxy and heresy in early Christianity, the Theologian draws on her scholarship in better understanding the centering force of the person of Jesus Christ. As the Interpreter provides an insightful reading of Genesis 1, the Theologian seeks to fit this into the broader Trinitarian creation-fall-redemption narrative. And when the Philosopher offers a refined articulation of logical arguments for the existence of God, the Theologian orders these in their proper place in proximity to the standards of the Christian faith—the Trinitarian creation-fall-redemption narrative centered on the person and work of Christ in his first and second coming.

Jerusalem Council

When the Jerusalem Council gathered to settle the question of whether Gentile converts to Christ needed to be circumcised and follow the Law of Moses to be saved, they didn't banish the basic doctrines of the faith to a back room. Instead, they appealed to aspects of the Trinitarian creation-fall-redemption narrative centered on the person and work of Christ to establish foundational principles for thinking through the issue.

It's easy to miss with just a casual reading, but Peter's address to the council incorporated the redemptive work of Father, Son, and Holy Spirit and focused particularly on the foundational doctrine of salvation by grace through faith in Jesus Christ. He noted that "God made a choice" that the Gentiles would hear the gospel and believe (Acts 15:7). God confirmed the acceptance of the Gentiles into the community of the redeemed by the evidence of the Holy Spirit who came upon them (15:8). They were saved not by works but by "the grace of our Lord Jesus" (15:11), purifying their hearts "by faith" (15:9). In fact, Peter used "creedal" language when he confessed, "*We believe*" (15:11). And he appealed to an article of faith that was believed, taught, and confessed by the body of Christ worldwide, thus carrying out the *task of the Theologian*.

CHAPTER 6

THE BURDEN OF THE VIRTUOUS

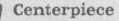

Centerpiece

The Virtuous serves as the conscience of the Table by attending to virtues of faith, hope, love, prudence, temperance, fortitude, and justice as well as beauty, balance, and proportion.

In both the Old and New Testaments, as well as in the early church and well into the medieval period, the walk of every man and woman was often considered in terms of two "paths" or "ways"—one of vice (wickedness, darkness, death, folly) and one of virtue (righteousness, light, life, and wisdom). The first-century manual for training new believers, the *Didache,* begins its instruction on virtue and vice by pitting these squarely against each other: "There are two ways, one of life and one of death, and there is a great difference between the two ways" (*Didache* 1.1).[1] The term "virtue" can be simply defined as "positive moral and spiritual qualities."[2] The opposite of virtue, of course, is "vice."

Virtues aren't simply principles to live by, rules to follow, or laws to obey. In fact, to confuse virtues with commandments or to conflate

---

1. Translation from Rick Brannan, trans., *The Apostolic Fathers in English* (Bellingham, WA: Lexham Press, 2012).

2. Millard J. Erickson, *The Concise Dictionary of Christian Theology* (Wheaton: Crossway, 2001), 215.

the virtuous life with dutiful obedience would be to completely miss the spiritual depth of the Virtuous. Karen Swallow Prior notes, "Because no number of rules or laws could cover every moral or ethical choice we face, virtue picks up where rules leave off. And where rules abound, virtue, like an underused muscle, atrophies."[3]

In classic Christian theology, a central place has been given to the triad of "theological virtues"—faith, love, and hope. The medieval scholastic theologian Thomas Aquinas gave three reasons why faith, love, and hope are called "theological virtues": "First, because their object is God, inasmuch as they direct us aright to God: secondly, because they are infused in us by God alone: thirdly, because these virtues are not made known to us, save by Divine revelation, contained in Holy Writ."[4] Because of Aquinas's great influence on Roman Catholic theological development, the three theological virtues have often been associated with Western (and especially Roman Catholic) theology and piety. However, no one can deny that the New Testament and early church placed a great emphasis on these Spirit-enabled virtues as the heart of the Christian life (Rom. 5:1–5; 1 Cor. 13:13; Gal. 5:5–6; Col. 1:5; 1 Thess. 1:3; 5:8; Heb. 10:22–24).

But these virtues are not the only positive moral and spiritual qualities enabled by the Holy Spirit. Paul refers to the "fruit of the Spirit" as those virtues that stand in opposition to the "deeds of the flesh": "But the fruit of the Spirit is love, joy, peace, forbearance, kindness, goodness, faithfulness, gentleness and self-control" (Gal. 5:22–23). Perhaps by starting with the virtue of "love," Paul regarded the rest of these character qualities as flowing from love as their source. He concludes, "Against such things there is no law" (v. 23). The term "such things" implies that Paul's list was meant to be only representative, not exhaustive. In fact, by surveying the New Testament, we see numerous positive qualities that fill the category of "virtue"—and even these shouldn't be thought of as comprehending the entire life of virtue.

---

3. Karen Swallow Prior, *On Reading Well: Finding the Good Life through Great Books* (Grand Rapids: Brazos Press, 2018), 34.

4. Aquinas, *Summa Theologica*, 1[2].62.1 (Thomas Aquinas, *Summa Theologica*, trans. Fathers of the English Dominican Province [London: Burns Oates & Washbourne, n.d.]).

Brotherly Affection (*philadelphos*)—1 Pet. 3:8; 2 Pet. 1:7

Compassion (*oiktirmos*)—Col. 3:12

Courage/Fortitude/Strength (*andrizomai/krataioō*)—
1 Cor. 16:13

Courtesy/Tolerance (*epieikēs*)—Jas. 3:17

Faith/Faithfulness (*pistis*)—Gal. 5:22; 1 Tim. 2:15; 4:12; 6:11;
2 Tim. 2:22; 3:10; 2 Pet. 1:5

Forgiveness/Forgiving (*carizomai*)—Eph. 4:32; Col. 3:13

Fruitfulness (*karpos*)—Jas. 3:17

Gentleness/Meekness (*prautēs*)—Gal. 5:23; Col. 3:12;
1 Tim. 6:11

Genuineness/Unhypocritical Action (*anupokritos*)—Jas. 3:17

Godliness (*eusebeia*)—1 Tim. 6:11; 2 Pet. 1:6

Goodness (*agathōsynē*)—Gal. 5:22; Eph. 5:9

Harmony/Agreeability (*homophrōn*)—1 Pet. 3:8

Holiness (*hagiasmos*)—1 Tim. 2:15

Honor (*semnos*)—Phil. 4:8

Humility/Modesty (*tapeinophrosunē/aidōs*)—Col. 3:12; 1 Tim. 2:9;
1 Pet. 3:8

Impartiality/Unprejudiced (*adiakritos*)—Jas. 3:17

Joy (*chara*)—Gal. 5:22

Kindness (*chrēstotēs*)—2 Cor. 6:6; Gal. 5:22; Eph. 4:32; Col. 3:12

Knowledge (*gnōsis*)—2 Cor. 6:6; 2 Pet. 1:5

Love/Charity (*agapē*)—2 Cor. 6:6; Gal. 5:22; 1 Tim. 2:15; 4:12;
6:11; 2 Tim. 2:22; 3:10; 2 Pet. 1:7

Loveliness/Beauty (*prosphilēs*)—Phil. 4:8

Mercy (*eleos*)—Jas. 3:17

Patience (*makrothumia*)—2 Cor. 6:6; Gal. 5:22; Col. 3:12;
2 Tim. 3:10

Peace (*eirēnē*)—Gal. 5:22; 2 Tim. 2:22; Jas. 3:17

Praiseworthiness (*euphēmos*)—Phil. 4:8

Purity/Sincerity (*agnotēs*)—2 Cor. 6:6; Phil. 4:8; 1 Tim. 4:12;
Jas. 3:17

Reasonableness (*eupeithēs*)—Jas. 3:17

Righteousness/Justice (*dikaiosunē*)—2 Cor. 6:7; Eph. 5:9; Phil. 4:8;
1 Tim. 6:11; 2 Tim. 2:22

Self-control/Prudence (*enkrateia/sōphrosunē*)—Gal. 5:23;
   1 Tim. 2:9, 15; 2 Pet. 1:6
Steadfastness/Perseverance (*hupomonē*)—1 Tim. 6:11; 2 Tim. 3:10;
   2 Pet. 1:6
Sympathy (*sumpathēs*)—1 Pet. 3:8
Tenderheartedness (*eusplanchnos*)—Eph. 4:32; 1 Pet. 3:8
Thankfulness (*eucharistos*)—Col. 2:7; 3:15
Truth (*alētheia*)—2 Cor. 6:7; Eph. 5:9; Phil. 4:8
Uprightness/Excellence (*aretē*)—Phil. 4:8; 2 Pet. 1:5
Watchfulness/Soberness (*grēgoreō/nēphō*)—1 Cor. 16:13;
   1 Thess. 5:6; 1 Pet. 5:8
Wisdom/Insight (*sophia/phronēsis*)—Eph. 1:8; Jas. 3:17

Various New Testament virtue lists—as well as the numerous mentions of specific virtues—move the Spirit-empowered Christian well beyond Plato's classic "four cardinal virtues" of wisdom (*sophia*), fortitude (*andreia*), prudence (*sōphrosunē*), and justice (*dikaiosunē*). The virtues of the Christian heart and mind result not only in new attitudes and actions but also in new patterns, habits, and lifestyles. Believers are to grow in God's transforming grace (2 Pet. 3:18). As they do, Christians grow more and more into the likeness of God, who is love (1 John 4:8), and who declares that love for God and love for others fulfills the Law and the Prophets (Matt. 22:36–40).

But how does *virtue* function in theological method? What does the Virtuous bring to the Table? Christian thinkers have long contended that virtue must function as the starting point, end point, and reference point of theology. As the starting point of theology, virtue is the right condition of the heart and the right frame of mind with which believers are to engage in discourse concerning God, his works, and his ways. As the end point of theology, virtue in the sense of transformation of the mind, will, and life is the practical goal of theology—not merely information, but transformation. As the reference point of theology, virtue becomes itself a nonverbal revelation of God in this world and a touchstone for helping us determine the validity of our understanding of his revelation. We will introduce each of these roles of virtue in turn.

?

FAQ

Wait—Aren't We All Supposed to Bring Virtue to the Table?

Yes! Remember, the eight characters at the Table are personifications of important perspectives and voices that need to be included in our discourse concerning God, his works, and his ways. In this sense, virtue should be a part of every conversation as described in these chapters. The Virtuous should be the close friend of the Interpreter, the Theologian, the Philosopher, the Minister, the Artist, the Scientist, and the Historian. Her whisper should always be heard in our ears, her words should always flow from our mouths, and her goodness should always characterize our attitudes and actions. While you or I might be able to get away with being primarily a Historian but not much of an Artist, each of us is called to don the character of the Virtuous.

VIRTUE AS THE STARTING POINT OF THEOLOGY

The second-century pastor Irenaeus of Lyons once reflected on the believer's reading of Scripture, asserting that a right understanding of its truth requires a right disposition:

> A sound mind, and one which does not expose its possessor to danger, and is devoted to piety and the love of truth, will eagerly meditate upon those things which God has placed within the power of mankind, and has subjected to our knowledge, and will make advancement in [acquaintance with] them, rendering the knowledge of them easy to him by means of daily study.[5]

Here we see the virtuous life at work in the heart, mind, and disposition of the believer even prior to opening the Scriptures. The virtues exhibited in Irenaeus's prescription include soundness of mind, piety, humility, and diligence.

The German Reformer Martin Luther also underscored the importance of virtue as the starting point for theological reflection. In his

---

5. Irenaeus, *Against Heresies* 2.27.1 (ANF 1:398).

preface to the 1539 Wittenberg edition of his German works, Luther emphasized the disciplines of prayer, (*oratio*), meditation (*meditatio*), and spiritual trials (*tentatio*). In doing so, he highlighted virtues like humility, diligence, knowledge, perseverance, and faith.[6]

Summing up virtue as the proper starting point for theology, we might do well to insist on four principles based on the authority of the Scriptures:

First, we must begin with the virtue of *humility*, expressed through teachability and prayer (see 1 Cor. 2:14; Eph. 1:17–19; Jude 20). Prayer admits our own inability and humble dependence on God's enabling grace. We should recognize that apart from the Spirit's work in our own hearts and minds, and through those teachers and fellow students in the church past and present, we will be lost in the dark.

Second, we must cultivate the virtue of *faithfulness*, expressed through belief and obedience (see John 14:21; 2 Tim. 3:16–17; Heb. 11:3, 6). We must nurture a disposition of responsive faith that takes God's revelation with utmost seriousness and sincerity. A ready willingness to embrace God's Word and to obey his precepts is presupposed in the pursuit of Christian truth.

Third, we must dwell in the virtue of *perseverance*, expressed through patient discipline (see 1 Tim. 4:13–15; 2 Tim. 2:15; 3:15; 2 Pet. 3:16). Though God enables understanding, faith, and obedience, this enabling work leads to our active and diligent participation in the activities that lead to growth. We must remember that fine-tuning our theological wisdom takes years, not weeks. We learn through trial and testing, instruction and experience.

Fourth, we must exercise the virtue of *prudence*, expressed through caution and discernment (see Jer. 17:9; Phil. 1:9; 1 Thess. 5:21; 1 John 4:1). Left to our own human weakness, emboldened by pride and stubbornness, we can deceive, be deceived, and deceive ourselves into all manner of falsehood. We should step carefully into the study of theology and its related fields of inquiry. We must never rush forward foolishly, jump to rash conclusions, or tear down the contributions

---

6. Martin Luther, "Preface to the Wittenberg Edition of Luther's German Writings," trans. Robert R. Heitner, in *Luther's Works*, vol. 34, *Career of the Reformer IV*, ed. Lewis William Spitz (Philadelphia: Muhlenberg, 1960), 285–88.

of others prematurely. Listening, thinking, meditating, discussing—these are the acts of prudence.

We see, then, that in numerous ways, God-glorifying, Christlike, Spirit-enabled virtue is the starting point of theology. As such, the Virtuous functions as the conscience of the Table, setting the proper moral and spiritual framework in which theology is to proceed. A sober disposition of the mind, a right attitude of the heart, and a sound orientation of the will are necessary before we open our mouths to discuss or attune our ears to attend to holy discourse concerning God, his works, and his ways.

VIRTUE AS THE END POINT OF THEOLOGY

Virtue is not only the proper starting point of theology; it is also the end point of theology. Theology is not just information, but transformation. Its goal is a life of love.

It is a gross misunderstanding of the theological task to believe that it terminates in correct thinking alone. Of course, all the participants at the Table think deeply and carefully about the subjects of their discipline. Content matters. Skill is essential. Knowledge is vital. But that knowledge can't be separated from virtue and character. Many of us have had the experience of interacting with a medical professional who lacked a proper "bedside manner," or a lawyer who couldn't be bothered to explain the contract, or an auto mechanic who had no patience with our questions. Virtue is even more essential for those engaged in theology at the Table.

Godliness—growth in Christlikeness and maturing in our walk by the Spirit—must be the focus. And we need this focus on godliness not simply because all forms of Christian ministry interact with people and represent the gospel in word and deed, but because one cannot truly know God without becoming more and more like him. Knowledge is holistic; it doesn't merely reside in the intellect but permeates the whole person and has an impact on everything she thinks, feels, and does. Our late teacher, Howard Hendricks, would regularly proclaim, "To know and not to do is not to know at all."

Virtue is the end point of theology. The Virtuous constantly taps on the Table and asks the question, "How does this theological truth conform us to the image of Christ?" and "How does this truth impact the way we love?"

VIRTUE AS THE REFERENCE POINT FOR THEOLOGY

Not only is virtue the starting point and end point of theology, but virtue is also a reference point for theology. As such, when virtue is perceived as the manifestation of the transforming grace of God in the lives of sinners, it's a revelation of the Word active in the world. Beyond this, virtue can also serve as a criterion for evaluating our interpretations of God's revelation. We'll look at each of these two sides of virtue as the reference point for theology in turn.

Virtue as a Revelation of the Word in the World

In a personal reflection on the doctrine of God's revelation, one of our seminary students wrote, "I know that God's Word is true because I am not who I used to be." Now, to be fair, this student had several other arguments for the absolute truthfulness and trustworthiness of God's revelation, but this one stood out. It brought out an important and often overlooked means of reflecting on God's revelation— experience. Yes, knowledge leads to transformation. But our *experience* of transformation leads to a deeper understanding of knowledge. Ellen Charry summarizes this idea well: "When Christian doctrines assert the truth about God, the world and ourselves, it is a truth that seeks to influence us."[7] She concludes, "It is not only the case that we must know God in order to love him. It is also the case that in loving we learn what loving is—indeed, how difficult it really is."[8]

The second century apologist, Athenagoras of Athens, put it this way:

Among us you will find uneducated persons, and artisans, and old women, who, if they are unable in words to prove the benefit of

---

7. Ellen Charry, *By the Renewing of Your Minds: The Pastoral Function of Christian Doctrine* (New York: Oxford University Press,1997), viii.

8. Charry, *By the Renewing of Your Minds*, 240.

our doctrine, yet by their deeds exhibit the benefit arising from their persuasion of its truth: they do not rehearse speeches, but exhibit good works; when struck, they do not strike again; when robbed, they do not go to law; they give to those that ask of them, and love their neighbours as themselves.[9]

That our virtuous lives are in some way a nonverbal revelation of God's grace and goodness is not a strange or novel view. Jesus himself urged his followers: "You are the light of the world . . . Let your light shine before others, that they may see your good deeds and glorify your Father in heaven" (Matt. 5:14, 16). As the light of righteousness shines forth from our lives, this Christlike virtue truly reveals God's glory to the world. What is this but a nonverbal revelation of God, his works, and his ways?

Another way our Christlike virtue reveals something of God, his works, and his ways is by the Spirit-empowered love believers have for one another. Jesus said, "By this everyone will know that you are my disciples, if you love one another" (John 13:35). Again, the truth that Christ is dwelling in and with his disciples is revealed by the preeminent theological virtue of love.

Thus, transformed lives of fallen, frail human beings that exhibit God-glorifying, Christlike, Spirit-enabled virtues are themselves revelations of God's working in this world. As the extension of the body of Christ in time and space, the virtuous is a revelation of the Word in the World.

At the Table

The character of the Virtuous represents qualities we all should have when we take a seat at the Table, regardless of the field or fields in which we have developed experience and expertise. More specifically, the Virtuous denotes fields related to spiritual or character formation such as spiritual disciplines, practical Christian living, and practical theology. In these ways the Virtuous necessarily

---

9. Athenagoras, *A Plea for the Christians* 11 (ANF 2: 134).

intersects with the labor of the Minister and the task of the Theologian. Also, the Virtuous incorporates the insights of moral philosophy and ethics (reasoned approaches to right and wrong) as well as aesthetics (the study of such things as beauty, balance, proportion, and fittingness)—thus overlapping with fields also associated with the Philosopher and the Artist. It should be clear that each seat at the Table bears the burden of the Virtuous, though sometimes particular individuals grace the conversation through focused attention to what is right, proper, befitting, and edifying.

Virtue as a Touchstone for Rightly Reading God's Revelation

One cannot understand divine revelation rightly without love permeating the process and the goal. Augustine wrote, "Whoever, then, thinks that he understands the Holy Scriptures, or any part of them, but puts such an interpretation upon them as does not tend to build up this twofold love of God and our neighbor, does not yet understand them as he ought."[10] And then, "So these are the three things to which all knowledge and all prophecy are subservient: faith, hope, love."[11] The apostle to the Gentiles expressed it this way: "And now these three remain: faith, hope and love. But the greatest of these is love" (1 Cor. 13:13). Love is greatest because God is love (1 John 4:8, 16) and because love is eternal. Faith and hope are fulfilled when their objects are seen and realized (Rom. 8:24–25; 1 Cor. 13:12). Love for God and others will grow in the infinite expanse of eternity.

Augustine says, "And, therefore, if a man fully understands that 'the end of the commandment is charity, out of a pure heart, and of a good conscience, and of faith unfeigned,' and is bent upon making all his understanding of Scripture to bear upon these three graces [Faith, Hope, and Love], he may come to the interpretation of these books with an easy mind."[12] In a very practical sense, then, the Virtuous insists that if the Interpreter's proposed interpretation of Scripture promotes doubt, despair, or hatred instead of faith, love, or hope,

---

10. Augustine, *On Christian Doctrine* 1.36.40 (NPNF 1.2:533).
11. Augustine, *On Christian Doctrine* 1.37.41 (NPNF 1.2:533).
12. Augustine, *On Christian Doctrine* 1.40.44 (NPNF 1.2:534).

that interpretation is simply wrong. He must go back to the text and determine where he may have taken something literally that was figurative, or missed an important context, or misunderstood a cultural background. If an interpretation produces unreasonable fear, unwarranted shame, or false guilt, it cannot be correct since perfect love casts out fear (1 John 4:18).

Augustine applied this "virtue principle" to decisions concerning whether a passage of Scripture should be taken literally or figuratively. He noted, "If the sentence is one of command, either forbidding a crime or vice, or enjoining an act of prudence or benevolence, it is not figurative. If, however, it seems to enjoin a crime or vice, or to forbid an act of prudence or benevolence, it is figurative."[13] He then gives an example from John 6:53, where Jesus said, "Very truly I tell you, unless you eat the flesh of the Son of Man and drink his blood, you have no life in you." On this passage, Augustine commented, "This seems to enjoin a crime or a vice; it is therefore a figure, enjoining that we should have a share in the sufferings of our Lord, and that we should retain a sweet and profitable memory of the fact that His flesh was wounded and crucified for us."[14]

Another practical application of the virtue principle as a touchstone for rightly reading God's revelation relates to what we will call the "fittingness" of a particular interpretation or doctrinal position in the overarching narrative of creation-fall-redemption. This is ultimately an appeal to beauty, proportion, balance, and purpose. This is more than merely interpreting an obscure passage in light of a clearer passage; it involves interpreting a passage in light of the big picture of Scripture and God's plan.

For example, let's say we're trying to determine if the vision of Revelation 21:1 of "a new heaven and a new earth" teaches a literal annihilation of the universe and replacement by an entirely new creation *ex nihilo*. A study of the language of "new heavens and new earth" in Scripture and its interpretation throughout history yields two options: (1) the annihilation and re-creation view, or (2) the radical renewal of

---

13. Augustine, *On Christian Doctrine*, 3.16.24 (NPNF 1.2:563).
14. Augustine, *On Christian Doctrine*, 3.16.24 (NPNF 1.2:563).

the present creation view.[15] Assuming exegetical and theological considerations could go either way, it's perfectly appropriate for the Virtuous to weigh in on the discussion and prompt us to ask the question, "Which view is more beautiful?" That is, does one view more fittingly complete the flow of the biblical creation-fall-redemption narrative? Of course, not every issue can be solved by asking this kind of question—nor can "fittingness" be the only line of argument. But at times it can help resolve some issues for which other sources of theology are unclear.

66 **Taking Your Seat**

Your spiritual formation and manifestation of virtue is a primary goal of theology. Your contribution to the spiritual formation of others in your community is also paramount. Whether you read Scripture, write music, help the poor, study genetics, build a church, memorize historical dates, or teach Sunday School, you must do so motivated with virtue and oriented toward virtue. And every informal or formal conversation about God, his works, and his ways should build faith, inspire hope, promote love, manifest the fruit of the Spirit, and nurture prudence, temperance, fortitude, justice, beauty, balance, and proportion. At no time in your participation in theology can you set aside virtue and sink into vice.

CONCLUSION

As the conscience of the Table, the Virtuous assures us that virtues of faith, love, and hope are the starting point, end point, and reference point for our discourse concerning God, his works, and his ways. Beyond that, virtuous living, manifested in numerous character qualities wrought by the Holy Spirit, is itself a revelation of the active power and presence of God through the abiding Word in the World—the communion of saints, or "holy ones," or—if we may—"virtuous ones."

---

15. See Glenn R. Kreider, "The Flood Is as Bad as It Gets: Never Again Will God Destroy the Earth," *Bibliotheca Sacra* 171 (October–December 2014): 162–77 and Michael J. Svigel, "Extreme Makeover: Heaven and Earth Edition—Will God Annihilate the World and Re-Create it *Ex Nihilo?*," *Bibliotheca Sacra* 171 (October–December 2014): 401–17.

Virtue, therefore, is the light that shines from the Word, it is a light to shine on the Word, and it is our light we are to shine in the World as we reflect the most perfect embodiment of virtue—the Word made flesh.

Jerusalem Council

When the controversy erupted over whether Gentiles needed to be circumcised and follow the Law of Moses to be saved, it was accompanied by "sharp dispute and debate" (Acts 15:2). The term "sharp dispute" (*stasis*), is the same term used for strife, disunity, or even an uprising or revolt. The ensuing debate, then, was characterized by virtues other than love, joy, peace, patience, kindness, goodness, faithfulness, gentleness, and self-control (Gal. 5:22–23). Rather, they exhibited vices of the flesh like discord, rage, dissension, and factions (Gal. 5:20).

When the Jerusalem Council gathered, there was "debate" (*zētēsis*), but no record of "sharp dispute" (*stasis*). And we can see from the brief record of the proceedings that through this open deliberation wherein opposing views were heard (Acts 15:5), the council shared openly and honestly, showing deference and respect for one another. Eventually, they had "become of one mind" (15:25 NASB), guided by virtues of love, unity, humility, and harmony. Thus, all members of the council bore *the burden of the Virtuous*.

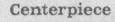

CHAPTER 7

THE QUEST OF THE PHILOSOPHER

> ❗ **Centerpiece**
>
> The Philosopher provides insight into fundamental questions of hermeneutics, truth, logic, worldview, and critical thinking necessary to better understand, defend, and articulate theology.

The Christian approach to knowledge and wisdom gained through reason, reflection, and study in the philosophical arts may be informed by the faithfulness of Daniel, Hananiah, Mishael, and Azariah when they were taken to Babylon and trained in the "language and literature of the Babylonians" (Dan. 1:4).[1] At the end of their three years of training for the king's service, they passed their examination with astonishing success: "In every matter of wisdom and understanding about which the king questioned them, he found them ten times better than all the magicians and enchanters in his whole kingdom" (1:20). Without compromising their faithfulness to God's revelation, the Jews in exile excelled in handling the wisdom of the Babylonians. Obviously, then, believers may learn from even the "worldliest" philosophies while maintaining the godliest perspective.

Though Christians often pit philosophy and reason against theology and faith, almost no theologian turns her nose up at the principles

---

1. In short, they excelled in an immersive cultural educational experience.

of logic when exploring God's revelation. Most Christian apologists point out rhetorical fallacies of false religions. Christian preachers, teachers, and writers strive to build their sermons, lessons, and outlines around sound arguments. And whether they know it or not, all interpreters of Scripture employ principles of interpretation informed by hermeneutics and undergirded by epistemology—both disciplines of philosophy.

? FAQ

What Is Epistemology?

Maybe "knowing-ology" might be a good gloss for "epistemology." But to be more precise, epistemology is a branch of philosophy that studies the nature of knowledge, its presuppositions and foundations, and its extent and validity. That is, it explores questions like "How do we know something?" and "What constitutes warranted knowledge?"

Granted, there is bad philosophy out there. The Protestant Reformers reacted quite negatively (and appropriately so) against what they saw as a hijacking of orthodox theology by the philosophy of Aristotle in scholasticism of the late Middle Ages. Rationalism and empiricism have fueled liberal theology since the Enlightenment of the eighteenth century.[2] If we practice philosophy as meandering speculations detached from the anchor of God's Word to the World and unguided by the rudder of the Word in the World, then such flawed philosophy can lead to a shipwreck of the faith.

So, what exactly *is* philosophy? On one hand, the Greek word *philosophia* is easy to define. It means, literally, "love of knowledge or wisdom."[3] On the other hand, philosophy is complex. In fact, one philosopher observes, "Defining philosophy is as difficult as trying to

---

2. For a helpful account of the historical conflict between philosophy and theology as well as an intriguing proposal for its resolution, see John D. Caputo, *Philosophy and Theology,* Horizons in Theology (Nashville: Abingdon, 2006).

3. Simon Blackburn, *The Oxford Dictionary of Philosophy,* 3d ed. (Oxford: Oxford University Press, 2016), 360.

define love."[4] This difficulty becomes apparent when we ask our students to explain the difference between philosophy and theology. The sources, methodologies, focus, goals, and presuppositions of Christian theology and Christian philosophy overlap. Yet in the following pages, we'll introduce the distinct role of the Philosopher as a partner who is not only welcome, but *necessary* for healthy theological method.

? FAQ

Doesn't Paul Condemn Philosophy in Colossians 2:8?

Doesn't Paul say, "Don't let anybody take you captive through philosophy"? Actually, the whole verse says, "See to it that no one takes you captive through *hollow and deceptive* philosophy, which depends *on human tradition* and the *elemental spiritual forces of this world* rather than on Christ" (Col. 2:8, emphasis added). The fact is, Paul himself cited pagan philosophers in his sermon at the Areopagus, demonstrating that he wasn't opposed to judicious and beneficial uses of philosophy (Acts 17:28). Though Paul condemned "hollow and deceptive philosophy," he didn't reject sound reasoning.[5]

THE PHILOSOPHER AS TEAMMATE, REFEREE, AND COACH

Arthur Holmes once noted two quests of the Philosopher: "The quest for clear understanding makes philosophy something of an intellectual conscience; the quest for a world view lends perspectives that guide the development of other phases of culture."[6] In other words, philosophy helps us think better and communicate more precisely and persuasively. Holmes regarded the Christian's function in philosophy as threefold:

---

4. Dallas M. Roark, *An Introduction to Philosophy*, 1982, accessed 30 December 2017, https://www.emporia.edu/socsci/research-and-teaching-links/philosophy-book/chp1.html.

5. Hubbard's warning is appropriate: "Paul cannot be said to be rejecting the study of philosophy per se in Colossians 2:8, but even so this passage contains an important caution that Christians need to heed. There is often only a very fine line that separates true wisdom from false wisdom, and that line can easily be blurred by those whose motives are impure" (Moyer Hubbard, "Is Colossians a Warning against Philosophy?" *Christian Research Journal* 29 [2006], accessed 2 January 2018, http://www.equip.org/article/is-colossians-28-a-warning-against-philosophy/).

6. Arthur F. Holmes, *Christianity and Philosophy* (Chicago: InterVarsity, 1960), 20–21.

1. A servant of theology who "will contribute to the discussion of theological problems old and new a penetrating insight," distinguishing truth from error, avoiding obscurity, and working toward systematization.[7]
2. A servant of apologetics, communicating to the world the viability of Christian theology with "a clarity of understanding, a consistency of argument, and a contemporaneity of expression."[8]
3. A servant of culture, giving voice to culturally relevant matters of aesthetics, epistemology, metaphysics, ethics, and history; as such, the Philosopher will stand as a "responsible member of society, sensitive in soul and alert to the bewildering conflicts of an onrushing history."[9]

To put the quest of the Philosopher in simple terms, we like to think of him or her as simultaneously functioning as teammate, referee, and coach.

Functioning as *teammate*, the Philosopher's insights drawn from the World of the Word advance theological discourse down the field. Not only does he provide astute principles of logic useful for constructing arguments and articulating truth, but he also contributes such fundamentals as the classic arguments for the existence of God, reasonable responses to the problem of evil, ready answers for apologetics, and the basic foundations of knowledge used in hermeneutics, history, science, and other fields of inquiry.

The twentieth-century conservative theologian Carl Henry wrote, concerning the longstanding view of the practical uses of reason in Christian theology, "That man's reason is a divine gift for recognizing God's truth is a main tenet of the Christian faith," which reason includes "forms of implication, deduction and induction, judgments and conclusions."[10] Four centuries earlier, in 1594, the Anglican divine

---

7. Holmes, *Christianity and Philosophy*, 35.
8. Holmes, *Christianity and Philosophy*, 35.
9. Holmes, *Christianity and Philosophy*, 35–37.
10. Carl F. H. Henry, *God, Revelation, and Authority*, vol. 1 (Waco, TX: Word, 1976; reprint, Wheaton, IL: Crossway, 1999), 227.

Richard Hooker spoke plainly on the necessary, positive role of sound reason in theology:

> Theology, what is it but the science of things divine? What science can be attained unto without the help of natural discourse and reason? "Judge you of that which I speak," saith the Apostle. In vain it were to speak anything of God, but that by reason men are able somewhat to judge of that they hear, and by discourse to discern how consonant it is to truth.[11]

Functioning as *referee*, the Philosopher may call "foul" when other contributors to a discussion play fast and loose with evidence, draw conclusions unwarranted by the arguments, or commit outright logical errors.[12] Logical fallacies and imprecise or inaccurate language can easily derail the conversation, lead away from the pursuit of truth, and result in nonsense or worse.[13] The Philosopher can hold members of the community to a greater fidelity to their principles and methods and can call for greater clarity of definitions and explanations. Thus, the Philosopher can strengthen the community's ability to make coherent, cohesive, comprehensive, and compelling arguments.

Functioning as *coach*, the Philosopher can train others in important skills such as logic and critical thinking. She can equip the Interpreter with a sound philosophy of hermeneutics, epistemology, and linguistics. She can instruct the Theologian and the Historian about the influence of various schools of thought on theological development throughout history, from Plato and Aristotle to Kant and Hegel. She can tutor the Virtuous in ethics, sharpen the Minister's philosophy of ministry, and deepen the Artist's aesthetics.

11. Richard Hooker, *The Laws of Ecclesiastical Polity,* Books 1–4 (London: Routledge, 1888), 197.

12. Regarding the role of philosophy in interdisciplinary dialogue, Holmes wrote, "It must not be supposed . . . that present-day philosophers are unconcerned about the subject matter of other disciplines. . . . They are concerned with the critical examination of scientific methods, of general concepts that arise or are assumed, of the interrelationship of various disciplines" (Holmes, *Christianity and Philosophy,* 4). Of course, other disciplines function in this way too.

13. A humorous illustration is the poem by Lewis Carroll. See "Jabberwocky," *Alice-in-Wonderland.net,* accessed 15 February 2018, http://www.alice-in-wonderland.net/resources/analysis/poem-origins/jabberwocky/.

As teammate, referee, and coach, the Philosopher plays vital roles at the Table. He or she provides insight into fundamental questions of hermeneutics, truth, logic, worldview, and critical thinking necessary for better understanding, defending, and articulating theological truth.

At the Table

The Philosopher signifies such a wide range of disciplines that it would be impossible for one person to master them all. So diverse are these pursuits that they necessarily contribute to the roles of every other persona at the Table. Related to the Historian, the study of the history of philosophy serves as the backdrop of most liberal arts programs and can be broken down into premodern (prior to 1700), modern (from 1700 forward), and postmodern (since 1900) philosophy. Relevant to the Interpreter and the Theologian, epistemology (the study of nature of knowledge, incuding its presuppositions, extent, and validation) and logic (applied organized principles of reason) are necessary foundations for sound hermeneutics (the interpretation of art, literature, music, or other forms of communication). Intersecting with the Scientist, the Virutous, the Minister, and the Artist, those engaged in philosophical studies may delve into the philosophy of science (critically addressing scientific presuppositions, principles, and methods), explore the nature of reality itself (metaphysics), explore the question of moral principles (ethics), or even study matters related to religion, politics, and economics (philosophy of religion, political philosophy, and economic philosophy). Practically, the persuasive articulation and defense of the Christian faith known as apologetics draws heavily on philosophy.

QUESTIONING THE PHILOSOPHER'S QUEST

The role of the Philosopher in theological method hasn't been without controversy in the history of Christianity. Though many early church fathers insisted that philosophers and poets taught truths consistent with God's revelation in Scripture, some had a rather negative view of the writings of philosophers.[14] This was especially the case

---

14. For positive examples, see Justin Martyr, *First Apology* 20 (ANF 1:169–170); Augustine, *On Christian Doctrine* 2.40.60 (NPNF 1.2:554).

when pagan philosophers engaged in unbridled speculation about religious and moral matters that bucked at God's revealed knowledge and will.[15]

One negative comment comes from the pen of the early church father, Theophilus of Antioch, as he compared the speculations of the philosophers on the origin of the world to the simple but profound narrative of Genesis 1:

> The utterances of the philosophers, and writers, and poets have an appearance of trustworthiness, on account of the beauty of their diction; but their discourse is proved to be foolish and idle, because the multitude of their nonsensical frivolities is very great; and not a stray morsel of truth is found in them. For even if any truth seems to have been uttered by them, it has a mixture of error.[16]

Ouch! It seems that Theophilus saw no place at the Table for philosophers and their "frivolities." However, his tone later softens a bit, and he takes a more balanced approach: "We must then give attention, and consider what is said, critically inquiring into what has been uttered by the philosophers and the poets."[17] On some matters— especially the origin of creation—Theophilus had little patience with the wild musings of the Greek philosophers and poets. On other matters, such as the nature of divine providence and attributes of divinity, the philosophers had something positive to contribute. In all things, care must be taken. Balance is needed.

Origen of Alexandria (c. 185–254) is frequently regarded as an example of unhealthy syncretism between theology and philosophy, which distorted the Christian faith. True, he allowed philosophical speculations to have too loud a voice where Scripture itself may have been quiet or silent. In theory, though, his theological method was intended to put truth obtained through a sound interpretation of Scripture in dialogue with genuine truths gleaned through reason. One of Origen's students recalled his method this way:

---

15. Holmes, *Christianity and Philosophy*, 21–22.
16. Theophilus, *To Autolycus* 2.12 (ANF 2:99).
17. Theophilus, *To Autolycus* 3.7 (ANF 2:113).

He deemed it right for us to study philosophy in such wise, that we should read with utmost diligence all that has been written, both by the philosophers and by the poets of old, rejecting nothing, and repudiating nothing... except only the productions of the atheists, who, in their conceits, lapse from the general intelligence of man, and deny that there is either a God or a providence.... With respect to these human teachers, indeed, he counseled us to attach ourselves to none of them, not even though they were attested as most wise by all men, but to devote ourselves to God alone, and to the prophets.[18]

During the medieval era, the scholastic theologians laboring in the European universities sought to construct a grand synthesis of knowledge, drawing from both revelation and reason, including authoritative teachings of church fathers, councils, and the pope as well as truths obtained by reason and philosophy. An ambitious—if overly optimistic—quest, to be sure! Nevertheless, some important warnings about excesses as well as nuggets of insight can be gained by exploring the theological pursuits of the Middle Ages. For example, consider the measured approach of Thomas Aquinas (1225–1274), who points to both an openness to the benefits of philosophy as well as caution regarding its limits:

Sacred Doctrine does make use even of human reason, not indeed to prove Faith... but to make clear other things that are put forward in this doctrine. Sacred Doctrine makes use also of the authority of philosophers in those questions in which they were able to know the truth by natural reason.... Nevertheless, Sacred Doctrine makes use of these authorities as extrinsic and probable arguments; but appositely uses the authority of the canonical Scriptures as an incontrovertible proof.[19]

---

18. Gregory Thaumaturgus, *Oration and Panegyric to Origen* 13, 15 (ANF 6:34, 36).
19. Thomas Aquinas, *Summa Theologica* 1.1.8 in Fathers of the English Dominican Province, *The "Summa Theologica" of St. Thomas Aquinas,* Part 1 (New York: Benziger Brothers, 1911), 13–14.

From a purely methodological perspective, this open but cautious approach to the insights of philosophical truth-claims based on reason, experience, logic, reflection, or analysis seems most balanced:

> We give diligent and watchful attention to the claims of philosophers of every kind, reading widely and deeply, though carefully and critically.
>
> We hold in suspicion or even reject the claims of those who carry out their inquiry based on worldviews and presuppositions utterly antithetical to the Christian worldview—such as atheism, pantheism, or materialism.
>
> We take care not to become enamored with any particular human philosopher or philosophical system, however well-regarded by the world; no philosophy should be allowed to usurp God's Word.
>
> We maintain our allegiance to God and orthodox truth and remain fully devoted to the revelation of the prophets in Scripture. We never outgrow our love for Christ and life of faith and obedience toward the triune God who has revealed himself to us.

When philosophy is used destructively, the problem is not with philosophy itself but with the perversion of its use. To be sure, radioactivity can cause cancer, but it can also be used to cure it. Uranium can be used in atomic weapons that destroy whole cities, but it can also fuel nuclear reactors that power nations. Unhealthy exposure to x-rays can lead to sickness and death, but it can also lead to healing diagnoses and treatments. Similarly, philosophy (and other applications of human reason) can be used constructively or destructively: as a friend contributing positively to theological discourse or as a fiend causing its destruction; as a handmaiden to theology or as a dictator over theology.

But this is true of any practitioner invited to the Table. The Philosopher isn't the only persona who can wield her unique position in a negative, destructive manner. The Interpreter can promote heresy through flawed exegesis or twisted interpretations. The Scientist can conform evidence to a theory of origins antagonistic to the doctrine of God as Creator. The Historian can rewrite or revise history in a way that reflects contemporary cultural values rather than the way things really were. Artists can sway people to immoral thoughts and attitudes. The Theologian can use Christian language and imagery but deny the essence of the Christian faith. The Virtuous can deceive whole communities into a contorted ethic that makes good evil and evil good. The Minister can damage the body of Christ by promoting practices that distract from—not lead to—the worship and service of God.

We're in good company inviting the Philosopher to the Table to help us reason well together. Practically speaking today, this would mean that we read widely—but also wisely. We ponder their ideas with fairness—but also with caution. Working through questions of legitimate synthesis of discovered truth is best done in community, where a number of critical eyes can help us realize when we're being either too critical or too yielding.

Origen of Alexandria declared, "We are careful not to oppose fair arguments even if they proceed from those who are not of our faith; we strive not to be captious, or to seek to overthrow any sound reasonings."[20] A little later he explained more fully, "If the doctrine be sound, and the effect of it good, whether it was made known to the Greeks by Plato or any of the wise men of Greece, or whether it was delivered to the Jews by Moses or any of the prophets, or whether it was given to the Christians in the recorded teaching of Jesus Christ, or in the instructions of His apostles, that does not affect the value of the truth communicated."[21]

In short, in responsible theological discourse, Christians must resist the temptation to dichotomize between sound exegesis and sound philosophy, between truths gained by reason and truths given by revelation. There are, of course, no truths gained by reason alone, since reason is a function of the creature interacting with the world that reveals her Creator. On both theological and philosophical grounds, we must reject an absurd method that pits truth against truth.

---

20. Origen, *Against Celsus* 7.46 (ANF 4:631).
21. Origen, *Against Celsus* 7.59 (ANF 4:635).

Rather, a classic Christian approach to philosophy in theological method has sought a patient and constructive dialogue between theology and philosophy, seeking an internally consistent, coherent, and comprehensive system of truth. Indeed, Christian history has frequently witnessed some theologians hastily rushing into an elaborate construction of a theological system driven consciously or unconsciously by philosophical schemes. But the past abuses of philosophy should never become an excuse for neglecting its proper use any more than the over-indulgence of food should lead us to opt for starvation.

66 Taking Your Seat

If you have no formal background in philosophy, we'd like to recommend a few basics. Start by familiarizing yourself with logic, especially treatments of logical and rhetorical fallacies. Being able to employ good arguments and to identify bad arguments will help you immeasurably in the pursuit of theology. Also, ask your pastor, teacher, mentor, or professor for recommendations of introductory works on the history of philosophy, ethics, aesthetics, and apologetics. From a very practical perspective, commit to calm, careful, and critical thinking about issues, taking time to gather facts, weigh arguments, and cut through less important considerations. Critical thinking skills are essential to constructive deliberation at the Table.

CONCLUSION

From hermeneutics to ethics, from logic to aesthetics, from philosophy of religion to philosophy of science, the Philosopher contributes to the discourse concerning God, his works, and his ways in the capacity of teammate, referee, and coach. She provides historical and contemporary insight into issues of fundamental importance. She trains conversation partners in logic, rhetoric, and critical thinking. And she challenges those at the Table to maintain standards of sound reasoning.

Yes, Christians have sometimes gone to extremes either by separating philosophy and theology into irreconcilable and competing pursuits—or by synthesizing philosophy and theology into a brittle system of subtleties and speculations. But a classic Christian approach to philosophy will avoid those extremes and take quite seriously the admonition to "love the Lord your God with all your heart and with all your soul and *with all your mind*" (Matt. 22:37, emphasis added) while heeding the warning that "the wisdom of this world is foolishness in God's sight" (1 Cor. 3:19).

Jerusalem Council

The Jerusalem Council engaged in "much discussion" to resolve the issue of whether Gentile believers must be circumcised and follow the Law of Moses to be saved. The term for "discussion" (*zētēsis*) can refer to an "inquiry" or "investigation," especially of a philosophic nature.[22] Though the discussion at the Jerusalem Council wasn't a philosophical debate, it relied on the methods and insights of philosophical dialogue in seeking a resolution.

The entire discussion involved arguments from a variety of sources. Here we see reliance on reason as they applied logic in their evaluation, analysis, and synthesis of their observations. Note the language of reasoned, rational deliberation. They met "to consider" the question (Acts 15:6). James declared, "It is my judgment, therefore" (15:19). Their conclusion and resolution "seemed (*dokeō*) good to the Holy Spirit and to us" (15:28). The term *dokeō* indicates a conclusion based on reasonably evaluated evidence. The entire council proceedings provide us with examples of *the quest of the Philosopher*.

---

22. See Henry George Liddell, Robert Scott, et al., *A Greek-English Lexicon* (Oxford: Clarendon Press, 1996), 756.

CHAPTER 8

THE PURSUIT OF THE SCIENTIST

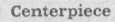

! Centerpiece

Gaining knowledge through the observation of natural phenomena, the Scientist explores God's self-revelation in creation to better understand and communicate theological truth.

According to the "Science Council," "Science is the pursuit and application of knowledge and understanding of the natural and social world following a systematic methodology based on evidence."[1] As a broad field with numerous sub-disciplines, science can be challenging to understand comprehensively. At first glance, it seems to provide a holistic approach to knowledge and understanding. At its core, however, science is a limited approach to knowledge about the world through observing how that world works.[2] In short, it focuses on the revelation of God in the World of the Word.

---

1. "Our Definition of Science," accessed 30 December 2017, http://sciencecouncil.org/about-science/our-definition-of-science/. It should be noted that we are using "science" in the modern sense; both the understanding of the term "science" and the methods used are historically situated. See also Sven Ove Hansson, "Science and Pseudo-Science," *Stanford Encyclopedia of Philosophy*, accessed 18 April 2018, https://plato.stanford.edu/entries/pseudo-science/.

2. In this chapter, we are adopting the view of scientific realism, the view that science is able to give a true account of the way things really are in the natural world. This is the majority view in modern philosophies of science. In contrast, a minority view, scientific instrumentalism, believes that science aims to describe the phenomena without concern about whether this is the

What can we say, then, about scientific method? One popular science website notes, "Science is a systematic and logical approach to discovering how things in the universe work. It is also the body of knowledge accumulated through the discoveries about all the things in the universe."[3] Thus, the methodology employed by scientists is rooted in observation. Generally speaking, scientists gather data by observing patterns and repetitions in the way the world works.[4]

Because God is a God of order and patterns, we would expect that his created world works that way. But this isn't a case in which God simply infused laws into the universe and then let it run like an independent machine, as Deists believed. Rather, God holds the world together by his presence and power (Col. 1:17). And in this universe God often intervenes and performs unusual, unexpected, and often unexplainable acts called miracles. Science, then, can explain many things about creation, but it can't explain everything.

Clearly, then, the Scientist, like all participants at the Table, begins with certain presuppositions without which science simply couldn't be done.[5] Furthermore, individual scientists and their communities and cultures lead to multiple starting points and worldview commitments: naturalism, theism, atheism, materialism, evolutionism, creationism . . . the list could go on. In short, science—even the "hard sciences" like physics and chemistry—begins with a kind of prior belief in certain unprovable axioms or rules, just as all fields of inquiry do.

Though scientists who are Christians must interact with scientists who sometimes have opposite worldviews, Christians approach the

---

way things really are. See Anjan Chakravartty, "Scientific Realism," *Stanford Encyclopedia of Philosophy*, accessed 18 April 2018, https://plato.stanford.edu/entries/scientific-realism/.

3. Alina Bradford, "What is Science?," Live Science, 4 August 2017, accessed 4 January 2018, https://www.livescience.com/20896-science-scientific-method.html.

4. This method is described variously, but generally as observation, gather data, form hypothesis, test hypothesis, analyze results, repeat the experiment. See Bradford, "What is Science?"

5. John Kekes writes, "Science is committed to several presuppositions: that nature exists, that it has discoverable order, that it is uniform, are existential presuppositions of science; the distinctions between space and time, cause and effect, the observer and the observed, real and apparent, orderly and chaotic, are classificatory presuppositions; while intersubjective testability, quantifiability, the public availability of data, are methodological presuppositions; some axiological presuppositions are the honest reporting of results, the worthwhileness of getting facts right, and scrupulousness in avoiding observational or experimental error" (John Kekes, *The Nature of Philosophy*, APQ Library of Philosophy [Totowa, NJ: Rowman and Littlefield, 1982], 156–57).

field with distinctive convictions. Among them is the belief that God is the Creator and sustainer of everything that is not God, and that there is consistency between God's revelation in the Word to the World, the Word in the World, and the World of the Word. The Christian believes that these three chords of revelation cannot be in conflict; rather, as we have asserted several times in this primer, contradictions are a result of flawed interpretations. The means of God's revelation—whether through Scripture or nature—are "essentially complementary."[6]

In 1615 Galileo rightly observed, "The holy Bible and the phenomena of nature proceed alike from the divine Word, the former as the dictate of the Holy Ghost and the latter as the observant executrix of God's commands.... God [is not] any less excellently revealed in Nature's actions than in the sacred statements of the Bible."[7]

Revelation in creation, the World of the Word or nature, must be distinguished from science, the interpretation of creation. Creation reveals God; science interprets creation. This means that creation and science are not in conflict with each other. There is often conflict between scientists, but these are disagreements about interpretation.

SOME ISSUES WITH SCIENCE AND THEOLOGY

Investigators from various fields of scientific inquiry labor to apply reason and experience in order to explore the glories of God's revelation in creation—even when they are unaware of (or even opposed to) the fact that God himself is the author of creation. Whether the scientist accepts it or not, "the whole earth is full of his glory" (Isa. 6:3). As Athanasius wrote, "God in His mercy had foreseen man's forgetfulness of the direct knowledge of Himself, and had provided also the works of creation to witness to Him."[8]

6. Walter L. Bradley and Roger Olsen, "The Trustworthiness of Scripture in Areas Relating to Natural Science," in *Hermeneutics, Inerrancy, and the Bible,* ed. Earl D. Radmacher and Robert D. Preus (Grand Rapids: Revell, 1967), 287.

7. Galileo Galilei, "Letter to Madame Christina or Lorraine, Grand Duchess of Tuscany, concerning the Use of Biblical Quotations in Matters of Science (1615)," in Stillman Drake, trans., *Discoveries and Opinions of Galileo,* (New York: Anchor, 1957), 182, 183.

8. Athanasius, *On the Incarnation* 12.1, in Athanasius, *On the Incarnation of the Word,* 2d rev. ed., trans. T. Herbert Bindley (London: Religious Tract Society, 1903), 26.

The principle of gaining wisdom from God's creation through a method of observation and interpretation is firmly illustrated in Proverbs 6:6: "Go to the ant, you sluggard; consider its ways, and be wise." The proverb urges the one who is lazy and slothful to watch the prolonged activities of the ant. From this observation, the observer is to gain practical knowledge that affects not only what the sluggard believes but also what he *does*. Likewise, Jesus encouraged his disciples to observe how God cares for the birds and flowers as an antidote to worry (Matt. 6:5–33).

In classic Christian theology, the observation of the natural world in order to draw theological and practical conclusions—and even to aid in our understanding of Scripture—has always been part of the discourse concerning God, his works, and his ways. Augustine once wrote, "There is also a species of narrative resembling description, in which not a past but an existing state of things is made known to those who are ignorant of it. To this species belongs all that has been written about the situation of places, and the nature of animals, trees, herbs, stones, and other bodies. . . . This kind of knowledge is serviceable in solving the difficulties of Scripture."[9]

Of course, this classic approach to the sciences as a fruitful means of interacting with the World of the Word has sometimes suffered. This was especially true in the modern era (since the 1700s), when the sciences were increasingly used not in the service of better understanding God, his works, and his ways, but in undermining them.[10] This dichotomizing between the secular and the sacred, the earthly and the heavenly, the temporal and the eternal, led many Christians to both distrust science and distance themselves from the fruits of scientific inquiry. This opened up the possibility of doing theology in dialogue almost exclusively with God's Word to the World (in Scripture), while virtually ignoring the Word who came into the World and the World of the Word (in creation). Others eliminated or ignored the Word to the World and elevated or isolated the scientific

9. Augustine, *On Christian Doctrine* 2.29.45 (NPNF 1.2:549).

10. See an historical account of this in David K. Clark, *To Know and Love God: Method for Theology*, Foundations of Evangelical Theology, ed. John S. Feinberg (Wheaton: Crossway, 2003), 260–73.

enterprise. This was a wrong turn, leading to the absurd position of pitting one means of revelation against another rather than receiving them as from a single divine source and as both useful to theology in their own ways.

For example, the nineteenth-century theologian G. T. Shedd too sharply dichotomized between the natural and supernatural worlds, making the field of theology concerned only with the latter and stating that the beautiful and glorious created realm—visible or invisible—is "not the proper home of theological inquiry."[11] Having accepted the dichotomy between natural and supernatural realms, Shedd proposed a method of theology that descends "from spirit to nature," expressly countering the alternative method of ascending from nature to nature's God.[12] Indeed, the contrary method against which he argues—subjecting the supernatural to what can be most surely known through the study of nature—is completely unacceptable in light of a classic Christian perspective on divine revelation involving the Word to the World and the Word in the World.

However, both of these approaches—ascending from nature to the spiritual and descending from the spiritual to nature—share the same flawed premise: that we must dichotomize between the two realms. If we understand the task of theology to be essentially incarnational, then in the plan and purpose of God through Jesus Christ, the creation both visible and invisible and the realms both "natural" and "spiritual" must be regarded as reconciled in Christ and thus reconcilable in the Christian mind (Col. 1:16, 20). Neither the fields that converse in the supernatural, religious, or moral, nor the fields that explore the natural, philosophical, or scientific can be neglected. Both realms—because in Christ they are really but one realm—are the fields of theological inquiry.

Another approach seen in the modern era is rooted is the perceived

---

11. William G. T. Shedd, *Discourses and Essays* (Andover: W. F. Draper, 1856), 13–14.

12. Shedd, *Discourses and Essays,* 14. Shedd writes, "The true method then of theological studies is to commence in and with the supernatural and to work outward and downward to the natural. The theologian must study his own spirit by the aid of the written word. He will ever find the two in perfect harmony and mutually confirming each other. The supernatural doctrines of theology must be seen in their own light; must bring their own evidence with them, and theology must be a self-supported science" (Shedd, *Discourses and Essays,* 22).

incommensurability of the natural and spiritual worlds.[13] The rise of methods, instrumentation, and theories from the sixteenth century onward seemed to grant modern science a newfound credibility that made its service to biblical interpretation less necessary. As a result, the interests of scientists shifted from Scripture to nature; nature became an object of inquiry unto itself, not a means by which God reveals himself. As a result, science employed methods that seemingly produced more stable conclusions than those produced by interpretation of the Bible. They were rooted in evidence and verifiability, not faith seeking understanding.[14]

Science should never be pitted against theology. Both disciplines start with some unproven convictions. Both are responding to God's revelation. Both are carried out by fallen creatures, and the presence of the Spirit of God in believers doesn't remove the impact of sin. And finally, practitioners of both need the insights of each other.

At the Table

The character of the Scientist comprises fields as diverse as mathematics, electrical engineering, medicine, and virology. This includes "hard sciences" like physics, chemistry, and biology as well as "soft sciences" like sociology, psychology, and cultural anthropology. It should be easy to imagine how such manifold pursuits would relate to other seats at the Table like the Minister and the Theologian. The persona of the Scientist also involves the foundational critical work of the philosophy of science (thus participating in the quest of the Philosopher) and the practical work of applied sciences like technology and invention (thus intersecting with the passion of the Artist). In conversation with the Historian, science includes archaeology—the study of ancient societies through physical relics, and in dialogue with the Interpreter, it would cover philology and linguistics (studies related to oral and written communication).

---

13. In the philosophy of science, "incommensurability" refers to "theories which, in a radical sense, cannot be compared" (James Logue, "Incommensurability," in *The Oxford Companion to Philosophy*, ed. Ted Honderich [Oxford: Oxford University Press, 1995], 397).

14. See Peter Harrison, *The Bible, Protestantism, and the Rise of Natural Science* (New York: Cambridge University Press, 2001).

SOME PRINCIPLES FOR SCIENCE IN THEOLOGY

Augustine of Hippo presents a better model for drawing on truth gained through scientific inquiry—even if it comes to us from unbelievers. He writes, "Let every good and true Christian understand that wherever truth may be found, it belongs to his Master; and while he recognizes and acknowledges the truth, even in their religious literature, let him reject the figments of superstition."[15]

Calvin expressed a similar thought: "But if the Lord has been pleased to assist us by the work and ministry of the ungodly in physics, dialectics, mathematics, and other similar sciences, let us avail ourselves of it, lest, by neglecting the gifts of God spontaneously offered to us, we be justly punished for our sloth."[16]

Note a few principles in these statements. First, the person engaged in such dialogue is a "good and true Christian"—one who is orthodox in his or her faith and virtuous in his or her life. As Solomon says, "The fear of the LORD is the beginning of knowledge" (Prov. 1:7). The ability to distinguish truth from falsehood is as much spiritual and moral as it is intellectual. The implication is that "ignorant and unstable people" (cf. 2 Pet. 3:16) will fail to discern the truth from science and distort it, just as they do the Scriptures. A Christian's engagement with scientific inquiry requires seriousness of thought, soberness of judgment, stability of doctrine, and sanctity of life.

Second, the person engaged in dialogue with scientific inquiry should remember that she is observing the work of the Creator. God is not merely the source of creation; he remains the master of his work. When Paul asserts that God's invisible attributes are visible in what he has made (Rom. 1:18–20), he is referring not merely to the origin of the universe but also to its ongoing existence. The present revelation is dependent upon the present existence of that creation. Paul elsewhere attributes the creation to the work of the Son, in whom "all things hold together" (Col. 1:16–17 ESV). The Scientist is watching

---

15. Augustine, *On Christian Doctrine* 2.18.28 (NPNF 1.2:545).

16. Calvin, *Institutes* 2.2.16, John Calvin, *Institutes of the Christian Religion*, vol. 1, trans. Henry Beveridge (Edinburgh: The Calvin Translation Society, 1845), 318, 319.

his master and the master of the universe at work. Therefore, the pursuit of the Scientist is an act of worship.

Third, the person engaged in this dialogue must work hard at his task. Knowledge doesn't come easy, whether one is learning the skills of language, historiography, philosophy, theology, or science. There's no place in the pursuit of knowledge for laziness or sloth. Christians can't afford a superficial dependence on Wikipedia articles, Google searches, or unreliable sources by non-experts. A responsible incorporation of scientific inquiry may require the hard labor of learning new vocabulary, reading broadly and deeply in scholarly books and peer-reviewed journals, and even earning an advanced degree in a scientific field.

? FAQ

So, If the Revelation from Science Says One Thing and the Revelation in Scripture Says Something Else, Which One Wins?

"Science" is not revelation. Both theology and science are responses to revelation, interpretations of what has been revealed. The propositional truth-claims from various fields of science must be regarded as "second-tier sources." If the contemporary scientific consensus says one thing, while the historical and contemporary consensus of biblical scholarship interprets Scripture to say something else, the rule of thumb is to side with the enduring interpretation of Scripture. Why? Because the distance between the inspired Word of God and our faithful translation or interpretation of that Word is much smaller than the distance between scientific evidence in the natural world and the scientific truth-claim. Yes, the truth-claims of *interpreters* of Scripture or their related theological statements are also fallible and subject to correction, but Christian theologians throughout history have generally felt it to be a safer practice to hold to an enduring consensus of biblical interpretation and theological expression rather than rashly surrender those to the ever-changing demands of contemporary scientific theories. Of course, at times, new scientific discoveries require a modification of theological conclusions.

Fourth, the person who joins in this task is in pursuit of truth—not opinion. Avoiding superstition includes rejecting any interpretation of the world not worthy of the God we worship and serve. This means that sometimes, in the dialogue between the truth-claims of science and the truth-claims of Scripture, the theories of science—however firmly rooted in the scientific community or popular culture—must be rejected. But it also means that sometimes, we will discover our most darling interpretations of the Bible are merely opinions we have exalted to the place of unquestioned fact. For example, scientific discovery has informed us that the earth is the globe that revolves around the sun; it is neither flat nor the center of the physical universe. We must never abandon the revealed truth of the Bible, but we must be ready to admit when our reading of Scripture was wrong. Galileo wisely noted:

> I do not mean to infer that we need not have an extraordinary esteem for the passages of holy Scripture. On the contrary, having arrived at any certainties in physics, we ought to utilize these as the most appropriate aids in the true exposition of the Bible and in the investigation of those meanings which are necessarily contained therein, for these must be concordant with demonstrated truths.[17]

Finally, the Christian dialoguing with science must maintain a proper balance. Though the World of the Word genuinely reveals God, his works, and his ways, we must not neglect the Word to the World and the Word in the World. Exploring any scientific field with depth will inevitably mean wading into waters often infested with some deceptive ideologies, hidden agendas, and non-Christian presuppositions. Prudence and moderation are necessary virtues. On the Christian's interaction with branches of empirical inquiry, technological arts, and scientific reasoning "found among the heathen," Augustine appropriately warns, "In regard to all these we must hold by the maxim, 'Not too much of anything.'"[18]

---

17. Galileo, "Letter to Madame Christina," 183.
18. Augustine, *On Christian Doctrine* 2.39.58 (NPNF 1.2:553).

66 Taking Your Seat

At least in the developed world, and especially in western post-Christian secular society, "science" is like a new religion and "scientists" are like the new priesthood. Today this has resulted in two errors you need to avoid. On one hand, you may be tempted to grant "veto powers" to the Scientist, capitulating to whatever the scientific community presents as "fact." Don't. Scientific theories are in constant flux, and it has never been wise to link our interpretation of Scripture or theological positions to the prevailing scientific theories. On the other hand, you may be tempted to simply jettison all science as irrelevant or even harmful to Christian theology. Don't do that, either. As a window (or at least as a microscope, telescope, or stethoscope) into God's non-verbal revelation through the marvels of creation, science can help deepen our understanding of God, his works, and his ways. Instead, strive to interact carefully, constructively, critically, and Christianly with the contributions of science. Read widely, but read wisely.

CONCLUSION

As the means by which we observe, interpret, and apply truth revealed in the World of the Word, the sciences are second-tier sources of knowledge about God, his works, and his ways. But as Bradford explains, "a law just describes an observed phenomenon, but it doesn't explain why the phenomenon exists or what causes it."[19] In short, science is limited to the observation of the world that is. It cannot ultimately answer questions of where things came from, where they are going, why they are here, or whether they ought to exist at all! Questions of causes, metaphysics, and ethics are beyond the scope of scientific method. Thus, in the same way that other participants at the Table need to hear the insights from the Scientist, the Scientist needs to hear from the others.

Science does provide disciplined, orderly, and beneficial propositions that may accurately reflect the nonverbal truth relayed in God's revelation. As theologians who are, by faith, seeking knowledge of

---

19. Bradford, "What is Science?"

God, his works, and his ways through the things he has made, ordered, and arranged, we should be eager to carefully and critically incorporate what can be learned from the insight of the Scientist.

Jerusalem Council

In seeking God's wisdom in the matter of what Gentiles must do to be saved and how they must live as followers of Jesus, the members of the Jerusalem Council incorporated considerations from what we would call "science" today. They drew conclusions from experience—inductive reasoning based on empirical data. They drew conclusions based on "how the Gentiles had been converted" (Acts 15:3). God "showed that he accepted them by giving the Holy Spirit to them" and by purifying their hearts through faith (15:8–9)—a fact testified by numerous miracles (15:12). By observing these facts and drawing inductive conclusions, they built their case step-by-step in a scientific fashion.

In addition, the members of the council observed that the Jewish diaspora had resulted in a large representation of Jewish people accustomed to certain practices that made it difficult to fellowship with Gentiles in keeping with the new vision of the church (1 Cor. 12:13; Gal. 3:28; Eph. 2:14–15). This became the basis for the moderate practical restrictions placed on Gentile believers (Acts 15:20–21). Today we would place these matters in the realm of sociology and psychology— *the pursuit of the Scientist.* Though discussed at an informal level, the council weighed the social considerations and the psychological effects of certain practices on the Jewish community when they determined the reasonable limits placed on Gentiles who were living with believing Jews in the church (15:19–21).

CHAPTER 9

THE PASSION OF THE ARTIST

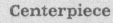

> ## Centerpiece
>
> Arts and culture contribute to a better understanding and articulation of God, his works, and his ways as particular means of revealing the image of God through human creativity.

A ndy Crouch has a great definition of culture: "What we make of the world."[1] The double entendre is intentional. Culture informs our view of the world in which we live, which gives us a grid through which we interpret reality. Culture also involves personal life experiences within our own particular time and place. The grid through which we view the world is also informed by our theology, our history, and everything that gives us the tools to perceive and interact with the world around us. In a certain sense, then, *everything* contributes to our cultural context, which results in our identity formation. Everything around us tints the lenses through which we view day-to-day reality. This dimension of culture—how we interpret the world God made for us—informs and is informed by several fields of science, from psychology to sociology to cultural anthropology. As such, that dimension of "culture" begins to lean into all the other seats at the Table.

---

1. Andy Crouch, *Culture Making: Recovering Our Creative Calling* (Downers Grove: Inter-Varsity Press, 2008), 23. The plural pronouns in this definition and what follows are intentional; culture making happens in community.

But flip Crouch's definition, and we have another dimension—culture is also a product of our creativity, a function of God's fashioning of humans in his image.[2] God formed and filled this world through a process of separating and ordering (Gen. 1). Then he planted a garden exceedingly beautiful (Gen. 2). In other words, through his own will, God made something out of nothing—the universe of time, space, energy, and matter. Such a making of the world is the work of God alone. But he took it two steps further: he fashioned something out of what he had made (this ordered earth), and then he glorified what he had made (the garden).[3]

Then he did something even more remarkable. God extended the blessing and responsibility to continue to form and fill this world to the human couple he had made. Thus, part of the way we manifest the image of God is by creating things from the raw materials of this world. God created coffee, cocoa, and cows. Humans created mochas. This aspect of culture, in which we continue to form new things out of what God has given, overlaps with the applied sciences, from engineering to statistics, from medicine to pedagogy.

Crouch also stresses that culture making is our Christian calling. We can't help but make stuff out of the world that God created. Whether what we make are ideas or worldviews or technology or art, everything we make begins with what God has made, including the culture maker. As Crouch puts it, "We make sense of the world by making something of the world."[4] In one sense, we are all culture makers; we are all artists. We all make artifacts out of the raw materials of the world. But there is a sense in which those who make music, paint, sculpt, invent technology, and create ideas are Artists in a fuller sense.

Culture making doesn't occur in a vacuum. Unlike God, who alone is able to make things out of nothing, humans begin with something. We aren't born into a culture-less existence; we're born into a culture. In fact, we are born into and nurtured within a variety of cultures.

---

2. On creativity in entrepreneurship, see Jordan Raynor, *Called to Create: A Biblical Invitation to Create, Innovate, and Risk* (Grand Rapids: Baker, 2017).

3. See John Dyer, *From the Garden to the City: The Redeeming and Corrupting Power of Technology* (Grand Rapids: Kregel, 2011).

4. Crouch, *Culture Making*, 24.

William Romanowski clarifies, "People are not born with a culture, a way of life, but are nurtured into one."[5] As we live, we regularly find ourselves in overlapping and even sometimes conflicting cultures.[6] Some of the elements of culture are good and should be retained. But seldom are cultural artifacts as good as they could be; we can reshape, reframe, and redeem those elements; indeed, we must.

Crouch suggests that we cultivate the good and add more good as we create, enabling humanity to flourish. He explains this metaphor: "Cultivation in the world of culture is not so different from cultivation in the world of nature. One who cultivates tries to create the most fertile conditions for good things to survive and thrive . . . Cultivation is conservation."[7] Crouch suggests we should also create new cultural artifacts as a way of redeeming cultures. In so doing, we're cultivating that which is good and worthy of preservation, and we're creating more good things for the good of the world. As a result, we make the world better, because "the only way to change culture is to create more of it."[8]

? FAQ

Isn't "the Culture" Bad?

If culture is "what we make of the world," and if it includes various social values, norms, patterns, and structures, then specific elements in a culture can be regarded as promoting or inhibiting virtue or vice. But the collective pattern

---

5. William D. Romanowski, *Eyes Wide Open: Looking for God in Popular Culture* (Grand Rapids: Brazos, 2001; revised and expanded, 2007), 60. He continues, "Beginning in early childhood we learn the ideals, norms, values, traditions, habits, customs, beliefs, and the acceptable behavior of a particular way of life. Worldview formation occurs when a person becomes conscious of that way of life."

6. Some of these cultures are regional, others determined by age, stage of life, or personal choice.

7. Crouch, *Culture Making*, 76–77. Crouch includes a helpful critique of several strategies which, he points out, have no effect on culture at all: condemning, critiquing, copying, and consuming (pp. 67–70).

8. Crouch, *Culture Making*, 67. He notes, "Underneath almost every act of culture making we find countless small acts of culture keeping. That's why the good screenwriter has first watched a thousand movies; why the surgeon who pioneers a new technique has first performed a thousand routine surgeries; and why the investor who provides funds to the next startup had first studied a thousand balance sheets."

of these elements that make up a culture and subcultures can't be thought of as entirely evil or entirely good; usually cultural forms and norms are neutral. Culture simply *is*, and we are inevitably part of it. We can't escape it, but we can utilize it for the purpose of theology and we can change it in a more positive direction.

CULTURE AS A SOURCE FOR THEOLOGY

How is culture a "source" for theological dialogue? Cultural artifacts (what humans fashion from the World of the Word) are particular, tangible, corporeal expressions of the image of God at work in human life. From Beethoven's majestic *Ninth Symphony* to the audio earbud we use to listen to it, our creations reveal the greatness and glory of God. And such artifacts that reveal the divine image through human imagination and innovation can come from believers and unbelievers alike. All humans are made in the image of God (Gen. 1:27; 9:6; Jas. 3:9), thus, all humans reveal him.

Expressions of human imagination and innovation—including artwork, literature, film, music, and other cultural forms—project truth about God, his works, and his ways, even when their image-bearing creators aren't aware of it. In fact, even intentionally twisted and distorted cultural artifacts find a place within the Trinitarian creation-fall-redemption narrative centered on the person and work of Jesus Christ. Remember that the story of redemption involves sin, rebellion, darkness, and tragedy. The gospel is the antidote to this need. Creative expressions can reflect these truths in powerful ways that capture not only participants' minds, but also their emotions and wills. Creativity connects truth to the heart and soul. Simply put, a fuller understanding of God, his works, and his ways can be mediated to us through a variety of cultural means.

Regarding the contribution of music to theological reflection, Augustine wrote, "We ought not to give up music because of the superstition of the heathen, if we can derive anything from it that is of use for the understanding of Holy Scripture; nor does it follow that we must busy ourselves with their theatrical trumpery because we enter upon an investigation about harps and other instruments, that may help us to lay hold upon spiritual things."[9] Like Augustine, we should acknowledge that, yes, non-Christians have used music in profane and destructive ways, but this shouldn't stop us from incorporating music into the service of theology. At the same time, just because we explore music for the purpose of gaining or communicating a right understanding of God, his works, and his ways, we're not obliged to fall headlong into an unhealthy obsession with "theatrical trumpery," losing sight of God's glory through the musical arts and focusing instead on human vainglory.

The German Reformer Martin Luther viewed music as a means not merely to convey doctrine in lyrical form but also to invite worshippers into a deeper encounter with God.[10] One scholar sums up Luther's perspective this way:

> A composer and lyricist himself, Luther valued the use of music in both the secular and sacred spheres ... He established congregational singing as an integral part of worship; and he wrote religious songs for recreational use. In his view, music in the church served as a *predicatio sonora*—a resounding sermon. It was to be valued not only as a vehicle for sacred texts, but also as being in itself a mirror of God's beauty and thus a means for reaching the soul directly with a message about God that is inexpressible in words.[11]

Culture can also provide us with ready-at-hand tools for discourse concerning God. Almost anything can become a means for exploring and expressing truth about God, his works, and his ways—human language, social and economic structures, educational and political institutions, literary and musical conventions, and other places and things. God's own revelation of himself through history and Scripture

---

9. Augustine, *On Christian Doctrine* 2.18.28 (NPNF 1.2:544–45).

10. Music also plays a significant pedagogical role because of the power of music as an aid to memory. See the use of music to renew memory in dementia patients, "Music and Memory," accessed 20 February 2018, https://musicandmemory.org/.

11. Richard Viladesau, *Theology and the Arts: Encountering God through Music, Art and Rhetoric* (New York: Paulist, 2000), 25–26.

proves that cultural forms are the means of disclosure. When God inspired Scripture, he used normal human language—so normal that the words are just as fully human as they are fully divine. He inspired psalms and proverbs in forms common to the culture of the ancient Near East. In teaching by parables, Jesus readily drew on the culture around him to explain deep theological truths. Apart from that cultural context—with its talk of camels and shekels—modern Western interpreters sometimes have difficulty fully grasping the message.

The implication of this use of culture for theology is that when we carry on our Table discourse concerning God, his works, and his ways, we must employ the culture—with its many subcultures—around us. Not *can*; not *may*; not *should*—*must*. We need to speak the language of our audience—their words, concepts, structures, idioms, and objects. To do this we employ cultural tools for investigation, articulation, and application. And we put the theological truths of Christianity in dialogue with cultural forms not merely to shed light on culture, but to shed light on our own understanding of Christian truth. Steve Turner puts it this way: "It's necessary to know the world. In order to address the world you need to be familiar with its concerns, triumphs, failures, and longings. You need to know its language because every nuance is important when communicating. You can learn about the world by traveling, reading, studying, talking to people, keeping your ear to the ground and taking a close interest in events as they unfold."[12]

Jesus is the model for a theology of culture. When the Son of God took on flesh and came to earth to reveal God to the world and to provide redemption, he came into a particular culture at a particular time and place. When he did, he was immersed in that culture. He spoke the same language as everyone around him, traveled by the same means they did, dressed like them, and lived as a first-century Jewish man. He also taught his disciples to immerse themselves in the culture when he described their work as salt and light. "You are the salt of the earth," Jesus said to his followers (Matt. 5:13). Among the possible comparisons in the metaphor is the use of salt

---

12. Steve Turner, *Popcultured: Thinking Christianly about Style, Media and Entertainment* (Downers Grove: InterVarsity Press, 2013), 232.

as seasoning.[13] Salt permeates the food it flavors. The salt is not the focus of the meal; rather, when the salt performs its task, it enhances the taste of the food. Christians make the world better merely by their presence in the world.[14] Similarly, Jesus said, "You are the light of the world" (Matt. 5:14). He explains the light metaphor's intended meaning when he goes on to claim that light is ineffective if it is hidden. Light is more powerful than darkness. Light drives out darkness. Light exposes the deeds of darkness (Eph. 4:8–14).

In his Upper Room Discourse, Jesus prayed for his disciples, that the Father would protect them from evil while in the world. His prayer was not that God would remove them *from* the world, but that he would protect them *in* the world (John 17:15). This prayer makes sense only if the followers of Jesus were to be immersed in the world, as immersed in it as he had been. Jesus made this point explicitly when he continued, "As you sent me into the world, I have sent them into the world" (17:18). Followers of Jesus are sent into the world as he was sent into the world—to affect and change the world from the inside, not from a distance; to be salt and light in the world (20:21). Only immersion seems to fit these metaphors well. And immersion means dwelling deeply in the world: swimming in its culture, speaking its language, and communicating through its symbols—its artwork, music, songs, and stories.

By walking in the Spirit under the lordship of Christ, the Artist recognizes that believers are not merely culture dwellers and culture engagers. As ambassadors of his kingdom and partakers of the image of God, we're called to be culture makers. In discussing the believing Artist's mission, Cameron Anderson notes, "I believe that the artist's calling is fulfilled when at least one of four human needs is addressed or met: supplying fitting design, advancing meaningful critique, generating palpable beauty or exploring ineffable mystery."[15]

---

13. "*Salt* was used as seasoning or fertilizer (BDAG 41 s.v. ἅλας a), or as a preservative" (NET Bible note on Matt 5:13).

14. "Salt" as flavoring of food also implies that our cultural engagement is with low or popular culture, not just the fine arts.

15. Cameron J. Anderson, *The Faithful Artist: A Vision for Evangelicalism and the Arts*, Studies in Theology and the Arts (Downers Grove: IVP Academic, 2016), 244.

At the Table

The persona of the Artist is, perhaps, the most fluid and flexible of the characters at the Table. On one hand, the figure embodies those actively involved in the creative, visual, performing, and fine arts—whether as pastimes or professions. On the other hand, it includes those who appreciate and explore arts and culture—whether connoisseurs of music or film, students of popular culture, scholars of cultural anthropology, or philosophers of aesthetics. The Artist stands for the passion of writers, composers, performers, inventors, carpenters, and builders—because all of these are engaged in radiating the creative image of God through forming and filling, ordering and ornamenting, innovating and improving. Thus, the Artist may contribute to the symmetry, balance, and proportion of the Theologian's system as well as the beauty, fittingness, and cultural appropriateness of the Minister's sermon or liturgy. Or the Artist may simply create beautiful things in ways that provoke curiosity and wonder, creating an atmosphere for embracing the burden of the Virtuous with mind, emotions, and will.

DISCERNMENT AND CULTURE

We know of no Christian so naïve as to claim that all cultural artifacts, forms, structures, and expressions are positive or even neutral. Just as individuals can project God's image in ways that twist and distort it so much that they cause harm to others, so can cultural forms be destructive. One immediately thinks of the culture engineered by the National Socialist Party in Germany during the Second World War. It's hard to say that the godless culture of violence, hate, and genocide wasn't "evil," maybe even a personification of evil itself. On the other hand, the very fact that we just named the wicked Nazi culture as an example of thoroughgoing human depravity at the societal level demonstrates that even godless culture can be used in the service of theological reflection. Bad examples—whether individuals or societies—serve to inform and instruct us in basic theological truths.

It is true, though, that most believers in the early church built a thick wall of separation between the world and the church, between culture and Christianity. They eschewed not only sporting events but also the theatre. Theophilus of Antioch in the second century reminded his readers, "We [Christians] are forbidden so much as to witness shows of gladiators, lest we become partakers and abettors of murders. But neither may we see the other spectacles [the theatrical productions] lest our eyes and ears be defiled, participating in the utterances there sung."[16] Real violence that resulted in suffering and death (as in the gladiatorial games) and gratuitous profanity and blasphemy in the theatre of the day pricked the consciences of the earliest Christians, who were striving for holiness. Thus, they tended to shun most forms of profane artwork, images, and many of the world's musical works and dramatic productions.

The question of whether Christians should watch fictional portrayals of profanity and violence in modern creative cultural forms is an important one today, for which there are no final answers. Almost no Christian believes viewing actual pornography is an option, but at what point does sexual content in a film cross the line from portraying reality in a way that is true to life and necessary for a story to simply tempting viewers to sin? Gratuitous violence is unacceptable, but at what point does a film cross the line from portraying the pervasive violence in the world or the re-creation of a historical event to desensitizing the audience to the horrors of violence? Again, this is hard to answer. For some, Paul's injunction answers the question: "Whatever is true, whatever is noble, whatever is right, whatever is pure, whatever is lovely, whatever is admirable—if anything is excellent or praiseworthy—think about such things" (Phil. 4:8).

However, this passage can't be taken as a blanket prohibition of seeing or hearing offensive content. Otherwise we couldn't read the Bible itself, which includes some raw immorality and offensive content. Rather, as Brian Godawa observes concerning Paul's thoughts in Philippians 4:8, "Ignoring the dark side is not at all what the verses are indicating... If we ignore truth's darker side, we are focusing on half-truths, and there are no better lies than half-truths."[17] He concludes, "Pointing out wrong is part of dwelling on what is right, exposing lies

---

16. Theophilus, *To Autolycus* 3.15 (ANF 2:115).
17. Brian Godawa, *Hollywood Worldviews: Watching Films with Wisdom and Discernment* (Downers Grove: InterVarsity Press, 2002), 199.

is part of dwelling on the truth, revealing cowardice is part of dwelling on the honorable, and uncovering corruption is part of dwelling on the pure."[18] The forthright, brutally honest, and sometimes even downright dark and dirty true narratives of Scripture prove this.

Viewing God in culture, making redemptive contributions through cultivation and creation, and communicating the truth of the story of redemption in a variety of cultures requires a great deal of discernment and wisdom. Rather than a set of universal rules that applies to all, wisdom requires the individual and the community to be in constant and consistent conversation about the process. William Dyrness reminds us that discipleship can take place in the world as it exists—a world full of evil, suffering, and sin. Good art will tell the truth, even truth that is difficult to hear or hard to see. Yet we need wisdom. Dyrness concludes:

> Discernment is not a matter of rules—always keep from this or that. Nor is it blanket permission to do what you please—this would deny the spirituality of art and imply, mistakenly, that art is simply a harmless hobby. Discernment is rather a skill that is learned over time and that varies from culture to culture. Moreover, it is a process that is learned and practiced in community, for it is together as the body of Christ that we come to understand what is good and what is not.[19]

Thus, he explains, we should "bear in mind that gaining discernment is a part of the larger process of becoming like Christ. Here, Scripture, prayer, and mutual admonition all play a critical role. A summary of these musings might be: Stay close to your brothers and sisters as you, together, stand close to Christ."[20] There is a greater discernment in the community than in the individual. Blind spots, rationalization, and perverted thinking are more easily seen by others. We really do need one another, maybe particularly so when dealing with

---

18. Godawa, *Hollywood Worldviews*, 200.
19. William A. Dyrness, *Visual Faith: Art, Theology, and Worship in Dialogue*, Engaging Culture (Grand Rapids: Baker Academic, 2001), 149.
20. Dyrness, *Visual Faith*, 149.

culture. In the same way that individual and private interpretation of the Bible leads to perversion, individual and private interpretation of culture leads to a great degree of perversion that can be spread more rapidly and broadly through media.

As culture makers, artists both redeem and create, repair and invent, fix and make artifacts which make the world a better place. They call attention to the fallenness and brokenness of the world and make a positive contribution. Their focus is not merely pragmatic, but they introduce glimpses of how the world could be a better place. They help us understand and put into practice the capabilities necessary for humanity to flourish. By imagining and portraying a more beautiful, just, and harmonious world, they create and re-create, bringing good out of the fallenness of the cursed creation.

66 **Taking Your Seat**

Culture isn't *the* enemy. Culture isn't *an* enemy. Culture isn't *your* enemy. Coming to grips with these facts is the first step in creatively making use of cultural "forms and norms" around you, perceiving the light of God's glory refracted through the creativity of his image-bearers (you, me, him, her, us, and them), and harnessing the power of "what we make of the world" to understand, live, and communicate the truth well. Make it a point to value the contributions of the more "creative types" in your community—artists, musicians, designers, and writers. Seek ways to unleash their gifts and skills in accomplishing God's mission, building up the body of Christ and bringing glory to his name. And seek ways to contextualize the mission in the actual culture in which you dwell. If you don't know how, ask for help.

CONCLUSION

In his book, *The Faithful Artist*, Cameron Anderson states his thesis regarding the vocation of the Artist and her relationship to theology:

I write fully persuaded that art, in its most exalted form, can be used by God to transform women and men, to extend his common grace to the world and to lead the church to worship. I believe with equal conviction that the content and character of contemporary art could gain the gravitas that it seeks if the artists who produce it were able to discover or recover the deep things of God.[21]

The passion of the Artist is to faithfully—but discerningly—infuse the world with beauty, which is the glory of God. As God's image-bearers, we are not ourselves the source of divine glory, but merely its reflectors in a dark world. As we infuse our music, stories, songs, paintings, poems, films, and worship with honesty and beauty, faith and love, mercy and hope, struggle and perseverance, we extend God's grace and truth to the world. We enculturate the heavenly message in meaningful earthly forms, and thus incarnate the truth for a world that needs its healing touch.

The vocation of the faithful Artist is not a frivolous use of time and fruitless waste of energy. Rather, "art is manifest in the world because we are the *imago Dei*. It cannot be otherwise."[22]

 ## Jerusalem Council

Had the Jerusalem Council met today, no doubt the members would have presented their perspectives with PowerPoint presentations and charts to aid in understanding. Perhaps Peter or James would have stood up, dry-erase markers in hand, and sketched out a diagram to summarize their arguments on a whiteboard. And maybe the decision would have been incorporated into a persuasive brochure to reinforce the theology of the council.

Though the council didn't have access to these modern-day cultural forms of deliberation and communication, we still see *the passion of the Artist* at work. First, we see Paul, Barnabas, and Peter use the cultural form of storytelling as a means of informing and persuading (Acts 15:3, 7–9, 12). Second, when they concluded their deliberations, the Jerusalem Council commissioned somebody skilled in the art of writing to craft a letter on their behalf. The letter was written according to the prevailing cultural forms of the day (15:23–29).

21. Anderson, *The Faithful Artist*, 5.
22. Anderson, *The Faithful Artist*, 251.

Besides the culturally defined medium of communication, the letter from the Jerusalem Council functioned in culture creation. Those Jews and Gentiles in the churches received and applied its culturally contextualized practical theology. No doubt this led to new approaches to worship, new expressions of faith that were neither Jewish nor Gentile but uniquely *Christian*. In this way, the role of the Artist both drew from culture and directed culture in ways that advanced the mission of the church.

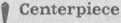

CHAPTER 10

THE LABOR OF
THE MINISTER

> ## Centerpiece
>
> Practical Christian living and ministry contribute to theological reflection by applying it in the arena of experience, resulting in a better understanding of God, his works, and his ways, and a better articulation of theological truth.

From the beginning of the Christian era, the ministry of the church has been established as the primary venue in which Christian theology would find its voice. Not in the academy. Not in the seminary. Not in the university. Not even in the home.[1] And not in the individual Christian. The church is the primary training ground and proving ground for theology—rendering *all* authentically Christian theology "practical theology." When Christ ascended to the Father, he didn't turn around and send a charter to a Christian school, or establish a philosophy of life, or set up an earthly kingdom, or found an evangelistic society or mission agency. Rather, the Lord Jesus built his church (Matt. 16:18; Eph. 2:20), and he "gave the apostles, the prophets, the evangelists, the pastors and teachers, to equip his people for works of service, so that the body of Christ may be built up" (Eph. 4:11–12). The health of this body is manifested when "each part does its work"

---

1. See Rodney Clapp, *Families at the Crossroads: Beyond Traditional and Modern Options* (Downers Grove: IVP Books, 1993). As important as the biological family is, the church is our first family (cf. Mark 3:31–34).

(Eph. 4:16). This "work" is not merely intellectual but applies theology to all life experiences. In community. In the church and in the society.

Among the New Testament writings themselves, three directly address the labor of the Minister—1 Timothy, 2 Timothy, and Titus. Often called "pastoral epistles," their principles apply broadly to all believers with ministry responsibilities. The tendency to separate or isolate ministers from laity, sacred from secular, and kingdom work from mere secular vocation is not found in the Bible. Rather, all sons and daughters of the king are involved in the work of the kingdom, in the process of making disciples (Matt. 28:18–20). As the workers of ministry carry out their Spirit-enabled labor—from the presiding elder of the assembly to the newest member of a congregation—theology *happens*. Returning to Ephesians 4, we see Paul's expected result of the proper functioning of the church's leaders and members carrying out their body-building tasks:

> ... until we all reach unity in the faith and in the knowledge of the Son of God and become mature, attaining to the whole measure of the fullness of Christ. Then we will no longer be infants, tossed back and forth by the waves, and blown here and there by every wind of teaching and by the cunning and craftiness of people in their deceitful scheming. Instead, speaking the truth in love, we will grow to become in every respect the mature body of him who is the head, that is, Christ. From him the whole body, joined and held together by every supporting ligament, grows and builds itself up in love, as each part does its work. (Eph. 4:13–16)

These things result from the labor of ministry:

Unity in the faith
Knowledge of the Son of God
Maturity in Christ
Doctrinal stability
Speaking the truth
Growth in love

We must underscore an obvious—but too frequently forgotten— fact that emerges from Ephesians 4: *all members of the body of Christ are ministers to one another.* The "Minister" at the Table is not the personification of an ordained pastoral or teaching office in the church local or universal, but a personification of all believers as they function in their capacity as a "priesthood of believers."[2] As we offer ourselves as living sacrifices in the service of "one another" for building up the body (Rom. 12), we contribute to theological discourse in the role of the Minister.[3]

MINISTRY AS PRACTICAL THEOLOGY

This immediately leads to the realm of what is often called "practical theology." By "practical theology" we mean more than simply "theological truth that is practical," that is, active. We have already seen in a number of places, especially in our discussion of the Virtuous, that God's revelation is not merely intended to be informative, but to be *transformative.* However, a common Christian approach to the relationship between orthodoxy and orthopraxy (right theology and right practice) has been linear. One author describes the linear approach this way: "Traditionally, evangelicals have assumed a linear model in which the flow of thought begins with the data of Scripture and history, moves to the interpretations of theology, and arrives at practical theology."[4] However, theology is a second-tier discourse concerning God, his works, and his ways; thus, our fallible understanding of God's infallible revelation puts us in a position in which we not only benefit from but *require* the feedback loop that comes from practical

---

2. This in no way minimizes the importance of the pastor as theologian. See Kevin J. Vanhoozer and Owen Strachan, *The Pastor as Public Theologian: Reclaiming a Lost Vision* (Grand Rapids: Baker, 2015), and Gerald Hiestand and Todd Wilson, *The Pastor Theologian: Resurrecting an Ancient Vision* (Grand Rapids: Zondervan, 2015).

3. For an inductive study of the "one another" passages in Scripture, see Gene Getz, *Building Up One Another* (Wheaton: Victor Books, 1976; new ed., Colorado Springs: David C. Cook, 2002).

4. David K. Clark, *To Know and Love God: Method for Theology,* Foundations of Evangelical Theology, ed. John S. Feinberg (Wheaton: Crossway, 2003), 190. Clark describes this view as *"essentially* correct," but also adds that "evangelical theology must listen to the feedback loop from practical theology" (p. 190).

Christian living and ministry. This hermeneutical spiral is the way all knowledge is gained and life change occurs.[5]

? FAQ

Even though I'm not Licensed or Ordained,
Am I Still a Minister?

Yes. The classic Protestant understanding of the church includes the doctrine of the "priesthood of all believers." This means that we are priests for one another, called to minister to others in the community of the church and to offer our lives up as living sacrifices on behalf of those outside the church who need to know the saving person and work of Christ. As such, we don't need to have formal training or ordination to fill the role of the Minister in theology. In this way, the voice of the Minister is somewhat like the voice of the Virtuous—everybody has something to contribute, though in the case of the Minister, there are some who do speak from that perspective of practical and missional theology with more years of deep and broad training and experience than others. The Minister's focus is the application of virture in the life of the community.

We believe a better approach to practical life and ministry and their relationship to the more academic approach to theological reflection is articulated in Keith Johnson's *Theology as Discipleship,* in which he shows "how the study of theology enriches Christian practice and how faithful obedience to Christ enables the learning of theology."[6] Rather than a one-way street from "academic theology" to "pastoral ministry," or from "doctrinal truth" to "practical application," these should be thought of as neighbors in the same cul-de-sac who invite each other over for backyard barbecues and borrow each other's tools. Their children play together, their families watch out for each other,

---

5. Grant R. Osborne, *The Hermeneutical Spiral: A Comprehensive Introduction to Biblical Interpretation* (Revised and expanded edition, Downers Grove: IVP, 2007), 22; "The major premise of this book is that biblical interpretation entails a 'spiral' from text to context, from its original meaning to its contextualization or significance for the church today." This spiral is seen not only in biblical interpretation but in the interpretation of all revelation. In short, learning is always a spiraled process.

6. Keith L. Johnson, *Theology as Discipleship* (Downers Grove: IVP Academic, 2015), 12.

and, in fact, *they learn and grow together*. Both are transformed (not just informed) through interaction with one another.

To some, this kind of relationship between orthopraxy and orthodoxy may seem like a failure to distinguish between the proverbial "cart and horse." Aren't biblical studies and systematic theology supposed to lead our ministry along the proper path? Or, if we want to state the logical relationship in a way that seems to maintain the honored place practical theology deserves, wouldn't it be more appropriate to consider practical theology as the "crown" of biblical-theological studies?[7] Or its chief end and purpose?[8]

No, the labor of the Minister in practical and pastoral matters is no less a vital source for our informed discourse concerning God, his works, and his ways than are the activities of biblical exegesis, scientific inquiry, virtuous living, or historical research. The Presbyterian Seward Hiltner comes closest to this model when he defines "pastoral theology" as "that branch or field of theological knowledge and enquiry that brings the shepherding perspective to bear upon all the operations and functions of the church and the minister, and then draws conclusions of a theological order from reflection on these observations."[9] In short, all the conversation partners at the Table are essential. Their contributions are not linear; they work the way a good conversation does.

"Pastoral," "ministerial," or "practical" theology should never have been thought of as separable from other sources and norms of theological method, nor as merely the end result of the method. Only by first separating "theoretical" from "practical" is it possible to treat one

---

7. Seminary curricula sometimes appear to perpetuate this approach, as students study exegesis, then systematic and historical theology, and conclude with practical theology and spiritual formation. A more integrative, organic, and dialogical approach would be preferable in light of our approach to theological method.

8. Alastair Campbell offers the intriguing suggestion that the separation of practical theology from biblical and theological studies and linear ordering is not actually a classic, conservative perspective, but a late nineteenth century development in a liberal tradition begun by Schleiermacher. He writes, "The relationship between practical theology and historical and dogmatic theology was seen largely as a deductive one, practical theology being understood as *applied* theology, just as, say, civil engineering is applied physics" (Alastair Campbell, "The Nature of Practical Theology," in *The Blackwell Reader in Pastoral and Practical Theology*, ed. James Woodward and Stephen Pattison [Oxford: Blackwell, 2000], 79).

9. Seward Hiltner, *Preface to Pastoral Theology* (New York: Abingdon, 1958), 20.

without the other. The result is lamentable. On one hand, it has often allowed us to harbor a cold and lifeless academic discipline unconcerned with people's spiritual needs; on the other, it has empowered a naïve but zealous religious activism uninformed by God's revelation. Clearly, neither of these is desirable as a custodian of God's revelation.

At the Table

It should be clear that the character of the Minister represents all forms of ministry in and out of the church, involving all believers with something essential to contribute to the building up of that body. Whereas the burden of the Virtuous focuses primarily (though not exclusively) on personal practical Christian living, the labor of the Minister assumes the corporate dimenions of prayer, praise, proclamation, and confession. In its skilled and trained iterations, the Minister includes such disciplines as homiletics (preparation and preaching of sermons), missiology (methods and means of activities like evangelism and church planting), and liturgical studies (including corporate worship and music). At the more interpersonal level, the Minister encompasses activities like counseling, accountability, Christian education, teaching, and creative expressions of sound doctrine in both written and oral communication. As such, the labor of the Minister necessarily intersects with every other persona at the Table, who all contribute to careful consideration of practical ways to build up the body of Christ by the power of the Spirit.

MINISTRY AS REVELATION

From a methodological perspective, the labor of the Minister cannot be thought of as a detachable "caboose" in the train of theological thought. Rather, the Minister takes a seat at the Table, not as a passive observer waiting to glean doctrinal prescriptions that she may then put into action at home, but as an equal contributor with the Interpreter, the Theologian, the Historian, the Philosopher, the Scientist, the Artist, and the Virtuous. The Minister comes with a set of experiences, questions, and a context in some ways different from the other participants. The other participants need to hear her.

This prominent place of the Minister takes seriously the biblical truth that the labor of the Minister is not simply driven by pragmatism. Rather, as a manifestation of the Word in the World, the body of Christ carries out its corporate ministry by the empowering of the Holy Spirit. In this sense, the church functions as the incarnation of Christ in the world.[10] Paul wrote to the church in Corinth, "There are different kinds of gifts, but the same Spirit distributes them. There are different kinds of service, but the same Lord. There are different kinds of working, but in all of them and in everyone it is the same God at work." (1 Cor. 12:4–6).

The Spirit of God—working through individual members of the corporate body for the common good—enables what Paul calls "gifts," "service," and "working." The first category, *charisma* ("gifts"), is often thought of in terms of supernatural abilities wrought by the Spirit of God through individuals for the purpose of building up the church in knowledge, wisdom, and faith.[11] The second category, *diakonia* ("service"), is the general term for "ministries"—labor offered on behalf of others. The third term, *energēma* ("activities"), emphasizes the divine enablement to carry out the edifying works, whether obviously miraculous or not.

Because of the parallelism in this text, a preferred understanding of spiritual gifts is that they are themselves acts of service and ministry. In short, they are not empowerment to serve, they *are* service. Spiritual gifts are not merely something we receive but what we give, through the Spirit, to the church, to the world, and thus, back to God.[12] This change in perspective shifts the focus from the individual to the body, from the parts to the whole; in short, it fits well with the goal Paul gives in Ephesians 4:15–16. Gifts of the Spirit are not what God gives to us, but what God gives to the church through us.

Whatever the body-building ministry exercised in the church,

---

10. By this we mean that the church is the body, the physical active presence of Christ on earth. We agree with the critique of "incarnational ministry" in J. Todd Billings, *Union with Christ: Reframing Theology and Ministry for the Church* (Grand Rapids: Baker, 2011), 126–28.

11. H. D. M. Spence-Jones, *1 Corinthians*, The Pulpit Commentary (London; Funk & Wagnalls, 1909), 418.

12. For the "traditional view," see Vern S. Poythress, *What Are Spiritual Gifts?* (Phillipsburg, NJ: P&R, 2010). For the view presented here, see Kenneth Berding, *What Are Spiritual Gifts?: Rethinking the Conventional View* (Grand Rapids: Kregel, 2006).

Paul is clear: "Now to each one the manifestation of the Spirit is given for the common good" (1 Cor. 12:7) The term "manifestation" (*phanerosis*) refers to something disclosed or revealed. Paul uses the term in 2 Corinthians 4:2 with reference to the "manifestation of the truth." Its verb form, *phaneroō*, is frequently used in reference to the divine revelation that comes to us by various means—by Christ himself (Mark 16:12, 14; John 2:11), by the created world (Rom. 1:19), and by the prophetic writings (Rom. 16:26).

Because the diverse ministries of members of the church are empowered by the Holy Spirit (Rom. 12:3–6; 1 Cor. 12:4–6; Eph. 4:7–13) . . . and because this empowering by the Spirit is an authentic "manifestation" or "revelation" of the Spirit in and through the church (1 Cor. 12:7) . . . and because the maturity of the body is seen when each member is doing her work (Eph. 4:16) . . . and because love is the evidence of Jesus's disciples (John 13:34–35) . . . the labor of the Minister is not only the end result of or a faithful response to God's revelation. The labor of the Minister is itself a source of nonverbal revelation of God's work by the Spirit.

The upshot of this is that PhD dissertations and Doctor of Ministry studies are of equal value at the Table. Studies on the history of revivals and awakenings can add to our understanding of evangelism and conversion. Missionaries' experiences with demonic forces and "spiritual warfare" in the field can provide insight into the wiles of the devil mentioned in the biblical text and recounted from church history. A seasoned pastor's hard-earned wisdom, gained through a life of suffering in ministry, can legitimately contribute to the body of theological knowledge preserved and passed down to later generations.

MINISTRY AS FAITH FORMATION

The labor of the Minister can have a profound personal effect on the theological convictions of believers. John Patton puts it well: "Christian ministry involves not only understanding what we do in the light of our faith, but also understanding our faith in the light of what we do."[13]

---

13. John Patton, *From Ministry to Theology: Pastoral Action and Reflection* (Decatur, GA: Journal of Pastoral Care Publications, 1995), 12.

God manifests himself to us personally in the life of ministry, because God, by the Spirit, shows up to enable, strengthen, and encourage us.

In 1960, Martin Luther King, Jr. described his own journey toward a deeper, more settled belief in a personal God. He came to this conviction not through logical arguments or philosophical musings, but through his tireless work in public ministry and especially through his agonizing labor for civil rights. He wrote:

> Now it [belief in a personal God] has been validated in the experiences of everyday life. Perhaps the suffering, frustration and agonizing moments which I have had to undergo occasionally as a result of my involvement in a difficult struggle have drawn me closer to God. Whatever the cause, God has been profoundly real to me in recent months. In the midst of outer dangers I have felt an inner calm and known resources of strength that only God could give. In many instances I have felt the power of God transforming the fatigue of despair into the buoyancy of hope. I am convinced that the universe is under the control of a loving purpose and that in the struggle for righteousness man has cosmic companionship.[14]

King's personal experience of God's protection and provision in the midst of great struggle was a revelation of the existence of God in his subjective experience.[15] When God showed up in Martin Luther King, Jr.'s life, it would not likely have had much persuasive or confirmatory power in the convictions of others. However, its potency for King himself cannot be doubted. In King's life—and in the lives of countless pastors and ministers—the labor of the ministry and the life of faith became not only a lab in which to test theological truth, but one in which to discover its greater depth. King said, "Some of my personal sufferings over the last few years have also served to

---

14. Martin Luther King, Jr., "Pilgrimage to Nonviolence," in *A Testament of Hope: The Essential Writings and Speeches of Martin Luther King, Jr.*, ed. James M. Washington (New York: HarperOne, 1986), 40. This article was originally published in *Christian Century* 77 (13 April 1960): 439–41.

15. For another example see Douglas Groothuis, *Walking through Twilight: A Wife's Illness—A Philosopher's Lament* (Downers Grove: IVP, 2017), where he tells the story of his care of his wife while she struggles with dementia.

shape my thinking... The suffering and agonizing moments through which I have passed over the last few years have also drawn me closer to God. More than ever before I am convinced of the reality of a personal God."[16]

King's namesake—the German monk-turned-Reformer, Martin Luther—spoke of the sufferings a minister endures as part of a "correct way of studying theology." He wrote that such "testing" is,

> ... the touchstone that teaches you not only to know and understand, but also to experience how right, how true, how sweet, how lovely, how mighty, and how comforting God's Word is, wisdom beyond all wisdom... For as soon as God's Word takes root and grows in you, the devil will harry you and will make a real doctor of you, and by his assaults will teach you to seek and love God's Word. I myself... am deeply indebted to my papists that through the devil's raging they have beaten, oppressed, and distressed me so much. That is to say, they have made a fairly good theologian of me, which I would have not become otherwise.[17]

Not merely doctrinal instruction but also theological reflection occurs in the context of worship, ministry, and prayer. The fifth-century motto *lex orandi, lex credendi* ("the law of praying, the law of believing") underscores this principle. Christians learn much of their theology through prayer and praise, music and liturgy, ordinances and sacraments, architecture and furnishings. The entire repeated experience of ministry becomes a venue for deep reflection and meditation on God's revelation and how it addresses the lives of believers—body and soul, mind and emotions, reason and will.

The labor of the Minister becomes paramount in communicating the faith to worshippers, thereby deepening their faith. Those engaged in leading a congregation in worship or shepherding a flock through life

16. Martin Luther King, Jr., "Suffering and Faith," in *A Testament of Hope: The Essential Writings and Speeches of Martin Luther King, Jr.*, ed. James M. Washington (New York: HarperOne, 1986), 41, 42. Originally published in *Christian Century* 77 (27 April 1960): 510.

17. Martin Luther, "Preface to the Wittenberg Edition of Luther's German Writings, 1539," trans. Robert R. Heitner, in *Luther's Works*, vol. 34, *Career of the Reformer IV*, ed. Lewis William Spitz (Philadelphia: Muhlenberg, 1960), 286–87.

must direct all things Godward, focusing the attention and affections of worshippers on the person and work of Christ by the power of the Holy Spirit. They create opportunities and space for a real encounter with Christ in Word and sacrament, pulpit and table, proclamation and consecration. At this point, theology is not just better understood; it is believed, received, and lived. The principle of *lex orandi, lex credendi*, as it relates to the close relationship between what we do in worship and what we believe and confess, must never be forgotten.

66 Taking Your Seat

Each of us is called to be a Minister in our families, in our churches, in our communities, and in the world. You have been gifted with talents and developed skills that make your contributions to ministry unique. Now build on these by stepping up and jumping in to carrying out the mission of growing and going. Find opportunities for formal training and informal experiences to sharpen your skills for more effective ministry. Then take time to reflect on how God is working in your life and the lives of those with whom you minister. Where might the Spirit be leading you? Perhaps you should consider more formal training in theology at a Christian institution or seminary. Perhaps you may be moving into a more full-time, long-term vocational ministry in the church or around the world. In any case, as you participate in discourse concerning God, his works, and his ways, don't neglect the insights gained through your own labor in ministry and the labor of others.

CONCLUSION

Miroslav Volf warns Christians that "contemporary academic and popular culture tends to subordinate beliefs to practices," relativizing theological truth and making beliefs merely a function of a way of life.[18] He—and we—rightly reject this approach. We cannot reduce "truth" to ways of life that will vary from culture to culture, religion to religion, or person to person.

---

18. Miroslav Volf, "Theology for a Way of Life," in *Practicing Theology: Beliefs and Practices in Christian Life,* ed. Miroslav Volf and Dorothy C. Bass (Grand Rapids: Eerdmans, 2002), 258.

On the other hand, an opposite error tends to prevail in much popular Christian piety—prioritizing belief over practice, separating the two, and reducing the Christian faith to the content of faith—confessional accuracy and doctrinal purity. Those who swing to this extreme would reject the notion that theologians can (or should) glean theological insight from life and ministry.

As in much theology, a balance and a tension must be maintained here. Volf rightly concludes: "Christian beliefs normatively shape Christian practices, and engaging in practices can lead to acceptance and deeper understanding of these beliefs."[19] Practical Christian living and ministry contribute to theological reflection by applying it in the arena of experience, resulting in a better understanding of God, his works, and his ways, and a better articulation of theological truth.

 ## Jerusalem Council

The doctrinal controversy that led to the Jerusalem Council began in the context of practical ministry—in this case, the pioneering mission of the gospel to the Gentiles (Acts 15:1–2). Do we circumcise the converts? Do we teach them to obey the whole Mosaic Law? The discussion toward a solution, then, took place not in a sterile academic environment among a college of highly credentialed scribes and rabbis. It took place in the church among those heavily involved in ministry (15:4, 6, 22).

Then, during the discussion, Peter offered their common ministry experiences as evidence of the Lord cleansing the hearts of the Gentile believers by faith (Acts 15:7–9). Likewise, Paul and Barnabas also relayed their personal ministry experience of God working signs and wonders among the Gentiles (15:12).

In the case of the Jerusalem Council, the key contributors happened to be those who were apostles and elders in the church. In other cases, the "Minister" involves the insight of lay people involved in ministry—even those of the congregation at large. We see this very early on in the church in Jerusalem, when the wisdom of the whole church leads to the selection of the "seven" in Acts 6:1–6. These instances demonstrate how the Jerusalem church relied upon *the labor of the Minister* as a vital source for theological reflection.

---

19. Volf, "Theology for a Way of Life," 258.

CHAPTER 11

THE VOICE OF THE HISTORIAN

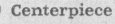

> **Centerpiece**
>
> To gain wisdom and insight from unfolding human history under the providence of God as well as from the wisdom of those who have gone before us, the Historian contributes to theology by giving voice to the history of doctrine, the history of interpretation, church history, and world history.

In a survey of the history of the interpretation of Scripture, one nineteenth-century Anglican theologian wrote, "A great part of the Bible is History, and all History, rightly understood, is also a Bible. Its lessons are God's divine method of slowly exposing error and of guiding into truth."[1] That is, the study of how men and women throughout history have interpreted (or misinterpreted) and applied (or misapplied) Scripture is itself a means that God uses to continue to guide and teach believers of every age.

As we dig a little deeper into the voice of the Historian in the Table dialogue, we'll explore a few areas of interest to theology: the importance of an understanding of the history of interpretation and application of Scripture, the meaning and importance of healthy tradition, the lessons to be learned from unhealthy tradition,

---

1. Frederic William Farrar, *History of Interpretation* (London: Macmillan, 1886), xii.

the great benefits and potential problems with creeds and confessions, and the powerful testimony of God through his providential acts in human history.

THE HISTORY OF INTERPRETATION AND HISTORY OF DOCTRINE

Few would deny that historical study—even of world history—aids in the interpretation of Scripture. Augustine wrote, "Anything, then, that we learn from history about the chronology of past times assists us very much in understanding the Scriptures, even if it be learnt without the pale of the Church as a matter of childish instruction."[2] Christians rightly insist that Scripture must be interpreted by giving attention to its original historical context—how the original words communicated particular ideas in a social, cultural, and religious environment within the historical period in which the text was originally written.[3] In this way, the study of ancient history of the biblical lands and cultures is directly related to the role of the Interpreter.

However, stepping out of the direct application of the study of the Bible's historical context, the voice of the Historian also contributes to our interpretation and application of Scripture as well as our understanding of the development of doctrine and practice. When we turn around and look back at the long history of believers who have read and lived Scripture in various contexts, some more and some less like our own, we can learn from them. They can teach us from afar through both good examples and bad examples by their wisdom and by their folly.

Aside from the history of interpretation, studying the development of doctrines and practices throughout history can help us discern those things that have always remained the same (the core of orthodox teaching and practice) as well as those things that have changed through legitimate development (like the formation of the New

---

2. Augustine, *On Christian Doctrine* 2.28.42 (NPNF 1.2:549).
3. See Grant R. Osborne, *The Hermeneutical Spiral: A Comprehensive Introduction to Biblical Interpretation,* rev. and exp. ed. (Downers Grove: InterVarsity, 2006), 37–39, 158–66.

Testament canon), illegitimate distortion (like the rise of heresy), and neutral traditions that helped contextualize the Christian faith for a particular time and place (like liturgies or worship styles).

From this perspective, the voice of the Historian can be a stabilizing force in an often-noisy brawl over individualistic interpretations of Scripture put forth by the Interpreter, overly confident commitments to one's dogmatic confessions asserted by the Theologian, or short-sighted, pragmatic ministry methods rushed into use by the Minister. A careful, critical, and constructive appreciation for Christian tradition will help Christians more responsibly engage in its community discourse concerning God, his works, and his ways.

What we are calling positive "tradition" is simply the course of healthy Christian interpretation and experience, which the church critically receives, carefully appropriates, and creatively passes forward.[4] Inherent in this definition is the fact that this body of believing, teaching, and living cannot be swallowed uncritically. Paul wrote regarding prophetic teachings, "Examine everything carefully; hold fast to that which is good; abstain from every form of evil" (1 Thess. 5:21–22, NASB). What was true of the assertions of prophets must also be true of the assertions of teachers throughout history. The apostle John wrote, "Do not imitate what is evil but what is good" (3 John 11). We must critically receive and carefully appropriate the teachings of the past, not blindly accept or blithely reject them. Positive hand-me-downs from the past include various forms and styles of worship, hymns, the works of the great preachers and teachers from church history, and anything else that served to pass on the faith from one generation to the next.

---

4. Gunton describes one model of tradition as "the actions of receiving, criticizing, and passing on" (Colin E. Gunton, *A Brief Theology of Revelation*, The 1993 Warfield Lectures [Edinburgh: T. &. T. Clark, 1995], 85). Similarly, at one point D. H. Williams calls tradition "that which the church has received, preserved, and carefully transmitted to each generation of believers" (D. H. Williams, *Retrieving the Tradition and Renewing Evangelicalism: A Primer for Suspicious Protestants* [Grand Rapids: Eerdmans, 1999], 9). Our understanding of tradition incorporates both *traditio passiva* and *traditio activa*, the former embodied primarily in Scripture and the creeds and the latter in the entire history of the church's ministry in the world in all its confessional diversity.

❓ FAQ

Aren't Protestants Opposed to Tradition?

No. The original Reformers embraced tradition handed down from pastors and teachers when it contributed to healthy Christian faith and practice. However, the Reformers were opposed to doctrines and practices handed down from church authorities when these doctrines and practices had no basis in God's authoritative revelation, displaced or contradicted God's authoritative revelation, or placed burdens of unnecessary beliefs or practices on Christians.

Such an inherited body of teachings and practices can provide stability to the Table conversation in a number of ways. First, the earliest tradition may serve as a guide toward a clearer understanding of apostolic intention in Scripture. Representing the first and second generation of the apostles' disciples, the earliest church leaders most accurately preserved the tenor of apostolic teaching, and thus their very early writings continue to serve as helpful guides in understanding Scripture and the original Christian faith. The second century father Irenaeus of Lyons wrote, "Even if the apostles had not left their writings to us, ought we not to follow the rule of the tradition which they handed down to those to whom they committed the churches?"[5] We have already seen in chapter 5, "The Task of the Theologian," how this basic content of the apostolic faith, known as the "Rule of Faith," can serve to remind every generation of Christians of those core truths of the faith, once for all delivered to the saints.

Second, a study of the tradition of the church invites to the Table the voices of the gifted pastors and teachers throughout history. Remember, Christ not only gave to the churches apostles and prophets (the authors of Scripture), but also evangelists, pastors, and teachers (subsequent generations of believers), all of them "to equip his people for works of service, so that the body of Christ may be built up until we all reach unity in the faith and in the knowledge of the Son of God and become mature, attaining to the whole measure of the fullness of

---

5. Irenaeus, *Against Heresies*, 3.4.1 (in Cyril C. Richardson, ed. and trans., *Early Christian Fathers*, Library of Christian Classics, vol. 1 [Philadelphia: Westminster, 1953], 374).

Christ" (Eph. 4:12–13). To attend exclusively to the writings of the apostles and prophets and to utterly neglect God's gift of the pastors and teachers would be like the Corinthian church accepting the seeds of the apostle Paul but rejecting the watering of the teacher Apollos (1 Cor. 3:6)! An interest in and respect for the thinking and writing of the godly and knowledgeable men and women of faith takes seriously Christ's promise that the Spirit would guide the apostles into all truth (and through them, the church indwelled by the Spirit; John 16:12–13; 1 John 2:27; Eph. 4:11–16). By means of that same Spirit, Christ would also abide with the church during its long journey through history (Matt. 28:20; John 14:18).[6] J. I. Packer noted, "Learning from the heroes of the Christian past is in any case an important dimension of the edifying fellowship for which the proper name is the communion of saints."[7]

Whereas a Christian must approach theology with a constant ear for voices from the past, an uncritical adoption of those voices has the potential of leading to distortion or gross error. However, by critically receiving, carefully appropriating, and creatively passing forward the contributions of believers from the past, we admit our own limited perspective and open ourselves to learning from those who have gone before. Jaroslav Pelikan aptly states, "Far from acting as a damper on theological creativity, this inclusion of the dead in the circle of doctrinal discussion acts as a stimulus to it."[8]

The Historian also gives voice to the classic confessions from the history of the church—not the words of a single voice from the past, but a chorus of voices from a particular historical community within the stream of Christian tradition. In this sense, the term "confessions"

---

6. Such passages seem to suggest at minimum that God's providential care for the church as the "bulwark of the faith" must mean that the church—however corrupt or distracted it became at various points in history and in various regions of the Christianized world—was prevented from absolute apostasy, and thus, the contributions of its doctors throughout its history ought to be regarded as the Spirit-led expression of this faith. To view any period of church history as a great trash heap between an absolute apostasy and some glorious restoration of the gospel does not harmonize well with Christ's clear promise to the Church that "the gates of Hades will not overcome it" (Matt. 16:18). See Williams, *Retrieving the Tradition*, 101–31.

7. J. I. Packer, *A Quest for Godliness: The Puritan Vision of the Christian Life* (Wheaton: Crossway, 1990), 16.

8. Jaroslav Pelikan, *Historical Theology: Continuity and Change in Christian Doctrine* (Philadelphia: Westminster Press, 1971), 160.

refer to formal or informal (written or unwritten) summaries of the Christian faith that serve as boundary-setters for the faithful. The informal expressions would be akin to the Rule of Faith of the early church.[9] The formal expressions would be various fixed, verbal articulations of the faith in classic creeds and denominational confessions. Williams rightly notes, "The Rule was not a creed, nor a formula, but an abbreviated body of doctrine wherein the genuine articles of Christianity were articulated."[10] While the Rule of Faith doesn't change, confessions grow and develop—putting in different words what the church has always believed, taught, and confessed, often with the addition of historically determined details that contextualize the faith for a particular generation.[11]

Historic confessions of faith play an important role in setting parameters within which the continuing theological conversation is to take place constructively. Confessions as particular historical expressions of the Rule of Faith, of course, must be understood in the historical situation in which they were formulated. Not all confessional formulae carry equal weight for all Christians. Some, like the ancient ecumenical creeds and definitions, are universal and have been generally received by all branches of Christianity (e.g., the Nicene-Constantinopolitan Creed of AD 325–381, the Chalcedonian Definition of 451). Others, like denominational confessions of faith, are provisional, articulating the theological standards for a particular theological tradition (e.g., the Lutheran Augsburg Confession, the Presbyterian Westminster Confession). Still others, like organizational doctrinal statements, are provincial or institutional (e.g., First Baptist Church's Doctrinal Basis, Dallas Theological Seminary Doctrinal Statement).

As second-tier sources for theology, such formal confessions can contribute both positively and negatively to the Table discussion. Positively, they provide healthy starting points and parameters for discussion, including a shared vocabulary and definitions. They contribute

---

9. Irenaeus, *Against Heresies*, 1.10.
10. Williams, *Retrieving the Tradition*, 88.
11. See Pelikan, *Historical Theology*, 109.

to unity and identity within defined communities.[12] They can anchor a community's growing tradition and prevent drastic and disastrous paradigm shifts, as occurred in the seismic revolt against classic Christian doctrine in the modern era with the rise of liberal theology. Confessions also reproduce and preserve the Rule of Faith, passing on the essence of Christianity from generation to generation in a stable form.[13]

Negatively, fixed and inflexible statements may reproduce and reconfirm idiosyncratic errors rather than orthodoxy. They can lead to the parroting of "Christianese" without real understanding of the meaning of theological terms. Some denominational confessions may close down dialogue if they're confused with first-tier means of revelation. They can be abused as standards of Christian fellowship, dividing smaller Christian communities from the larger body of Christ. The more drastically confessions depart from the historical Rule of Faith, the more these negative effects manifest themselves in the theological dialogue.

The Historian contributes to theological method in a variety of ways. Biographies, accounts of turning points in history, evaluations of backgrounds and cultural settings, and summaries and surveys of revivals and moves of the Spirit are all in the purview of the Historian. The Historian also deals with ethical concerns such as slavery, racism, sexism, and human trafficking. Sometimes the voice of the Historian can point out blind spots in the church, reminding us of vital doctrinal and practical matters long neglected.[14] Other times the voice of the Historian can suggest solutions to contemporary problems retrieved through the insights of those in the past. And frequently throughout history, the Historian's words have inspired fresh conviction and renewed confession, leading to revival and reformation.

---

12. George A. Lindbeck writes, "A religious body cannot exist as a recognizably distinctive collectivity unless it has some beliefs and/or practices by which it can be identified" (*The Nature of Doctrine: Religion and Theology in a Postliberal Age* [Philadelphia: Westminster Press, 1984], 74).

13. See Williams, *Retrieving the Tradition*, 13.

14. For examples of blind spots, see Sandra Glahn, ed., *Vindicating the Vixens: Revisiting Sexualized, Vilified, and Marginalized Women of the Bible* (Grand Rapids: Kregel, 2017). See also Anthony B. Bradley, *Liberating Black Theology: The Bible and the Black Experience in America* (Nashville: Crossway, 2010).

At the Table

The figure of the Historian incorporates a wide range of fields, some of which directly contribute to—or are informed by—other disciplines at the Table. The fields of historical theology, church history, and the history of doctrine greatly impact the task of the Theologian. The study of historiography (the research, analysis, synthesis, and presentation of history) and the philosophy of history draw on the quest of the Philosopher. The history of interpretation, world history, and the history of religions overlap significantly with the role of the Interpreter. The history of liturgy and worship can play a significant part in the reflection and practical application of the Minister. Art history informs the Artist and biography inspires the Virtuous. Whether we are individuals reading history, students studying history, or scholars writing history, the goal for the believer at the Table is not merely to procure information but to promote transformation.

A DISTINCTLY CHRISTIAN APPROACH TO WORLD HISTORY

If historians are all working with the same documentary and archaeological facts, what makes a Christian approach to history unique? How does the faithful Historian understand the events of world history in a way that discerns her role in revealing both the World of the Word as well as the Word in the World?

God's Providence over the Beginning, Middle, and End of History

The first distinctive of a Christian reading of history is the view that world history had a beginning and will have a definite end, between which humanity progresses toward its goal. This "alpha" and "omega" of human history gives meaning to the entire chain of events in between.[15] Many modern historians deny that there ever was an actual, discernible beginning in any meaningful sense.[16] Or they

---

15. Gerhard Sauter, *The Question of Meaning: A Theological and Philosophical Orientation*, trans. Geoffrey W. Bromiley (Grand Rapids: Eerdmans, 1995), 112–13.

16. See Ernst Breisach, *Historiography: Ancient, Medieval, and Modern*, 3rd ed. (Chicago: University of Chicago Press, 2007).

shrug their shoulders at any meaningful climax toward which humanity is progressing. However, a Christian approach to history takes into
account the fact that this universe was fashioned with a plan in the
mind of God, which included a purpose for humanity that drives history toward a future realization of that purpose.[17]

Because there was an intentional creation and an intended purpose, a Christian ought to reckon that history is being steered toward
that purpose by the sovereign power of God.[18] This has traditionally
included the notion of "divine providence"—God's activity in shepherding cosmic and human history. This involves the perspective
that the steps and stages in the unfolding of human history follow
an ordered path and that the parts are subsumed within a predeter-
mined whole.[19]

For some non-Christian historians and philosophers, the concept
of God's plan and providence was replaced by the notion of human
progress, which "enabled them to feel that the wheels of this universe
were not merely revolving and grinding to no purpose: they were busy
manufacturing something that was higher than the individual purposes of living men."[20] Historians often abandon a notion of providence in favor of human freedom; the former is sometimes regarded as
"religious" while the latter is "secular." However, the two—providence
and freedom—need not be regarded as incompatible. The study of the
free choices of individuals and peoples must be seen by the Christian
as the mysterious outworking of God's plan. In delving into this mystery, the Historian must dialogue with the Philosopher, the Theologian, and the Virtuous to avoid extremes and maintain balance
and perspective.

---

17. See Wolfhart Pannenberg, *Systematic Theology*, vol. 1, trans. Geoffrey W. Bromiley
(Grand Rapids: Eerdmans, 1991), 387.

18. See the discussion on traditional and modern views of providence in Langdon Gilkey,
Reaping the Whirlwind: A Christian Interpretation of History (New York: Seabury, 1976),
159–318.

19. This notion has from the beginning expressed itself in some sort of model of the suc-
cession of ages or stages in history, but a history that maintains its unity under the providence
of God. Cf. Auguste Luneau, *L'histoire du salut chez les Pères de l'Eglise: la doctrine des ages du
monde*, Théologie Historique, ed. Jean Daniélou (Paris: Beauchesne, 1964), 412–25.

20. Herbert Butterfield, *The Origins of History*, ed. Adam Watson (New York: Basic Books,
1981), 219.

History's Christological Center and Redemptive End

Throughout the history of the Hebrew and Christian traditions, attempts have been made at synthesizing the course of historical events into a unified whole. Often this was done by means of epochs, ages, successive empires, dispensations, or covenants.[21] These various models sought to present—at both the micro and macro levels—the flow of human history in light of the sovereign plan of God. Regardless of any schemes of universal history, however, Christians must see the grand narrative of creation's story as properly interpreted through the centrality of Christ and his incarnation.

E. C. Rust writes:

> The Christian Church is the heir to this Jewish faith, gathering up its vision in Jesus, and declaring that all history centres in Him and His redemptive work. St. Augustine gave classical expression to this view of history in his *Civitas Dei*, and through the centuries Christian men have clung to the faith that there is a history of the world, a history which is not a collection of the histories of separate nations and successive cultures, but which is a unity knit together by the purpose of God as revealed in Jesus Christ. It may truly be said that one of the gifts of Christianity to the world is the concept of world history.[22]

The Christian ought to view the incarnation of Christ not merely as the fulfillment of history,[23] nor as simply the grounding of the Christian faith in history,[24] but also as the means and promise of future fulfillment of God's revealed plan and purpose. In the midst of this fulfillment and promise is the work of creation, redemption, and

---

21. For a discussion of these various models, see in G. I. Davies, "Apocalyptic and Historiography," *Journal for the Study of the Old Testament* 5 (1978): 15–28. Compare Robert G. Hall, *Revealed Histories: Techniques for Ancient Jewish and Christian Historiography*, Journal for the Study of the Pseudepigrapha Supplement Series, vol. 6, ed. James H. Charlesworth (Sheffield: JSOT Press, 1991). In the latter work, the emphasis is on the understanding or interpretation of the past by means of special revelation.

22. E. C. Rust, *The Christian Understanding of History* (London: Lutterworth, 1946), 18.

23. Hans Urs von Balthasar, *A Theology of History* (New York: Sheed and Ward, 1963), 57–58.

24. Ronald H. Nash, *The Meaning of History* (Nashville: Broadman & Holman, 1998), 18.

restoration.[25] Wolfhart Pannenberg writes, "For primitive Christianity ... the dawning of these events in the person of Jesus not only initiated the definitive revelation of God but in a closely related manner showed what is the goal of the divine counsel (Eph. 1:9–10)."[26]

Thus, the Christian Historian cannot assert a great dichotomy between a so-called "secular" history of the world and a "sacred" history of redemption. We can't maintain an irreconcilable difference between God's work among his redeemed people and God's work in the rest of human history. All stages of human history are part of God's plan of redemption, moving the whole creation from the fall from paradise to the intended restoration. And this is true whether the Historian is studying the development of doctrine in the Christian tradition or the causes and results of the American Civil War. God is at work redemptively in human history.

Romans 8 gives us a glimpse of the universal implications of God's work of redemption. Not only is all creation partaking of the frustration of the fallen condition, but all creation also groans for the restoration. Furthermore, all things (in this context, presumably all events and acts in history regardless of apparent insignificance) "work together for good" (Rom. 8:28, NASB). That is, all individual events and occurrences are moving history forward and affecting the progressive redemption of individuals and nations in this interim stage while also advancing creation toward the goal of restoration. Similarly, in Colossians 1:15–20, Paul declares that the Son is the Creator of all things and the one through whom God will "reconcile to himself all things, whether things on earth or things in heaven."

In this light, the object of Christian historical study is not to be limited merely to a biblical or theological "history of redemption," but it must include the history of humanity in general. The unfolding of history is the progressive unveiling of God, his works, and his ways. Yes, the events of history must be interpreted by fallen, fallible humans in light of God's inspired verbal revelation (the Word to the World) and his revelation through Christ (the Word in the World).

---

25. John McIntyre, *The Christian Doctrine of History* (Grand Rapids: Eerdmans, 1957), 45–93.

26. Pannenberg, *Systematic Theology*, 1:441.

But history—the progressive outworking of God's plan for the World of the Word—is an authentic means of nonverbal revelation.

The Christian Practice of History

How does the distinctly Christian view of history affect her actual *practice* of history?

First, the Historian should be thorough, honest, and rigorous in her application of methodology and treatment of evidence. While historians must always be willing to correct misrepresentations of the past in historical studies, no Christian should ever be found guilty of agenda-driven "revisionist history" in a form that simply promotes self-serving propaganda.[27] While acknowledging the limitations brought on by one's particular historical context as well as general human frailty and sin, the Christian Historian must aim for truth as the standard of self-criticism. This doesn't mean that Christians must strive to "fit in" to the narratives or consensus of broader historical studies at all costs. But it does mean that the Historian must contribute to her guild and exercise her craft faithfully.

Second, the Historian should interact with scholars and insights from all philosophical and theological perspectives.[28] The careful and critical interaction with non-Christian insights can serve as both a curative of our own limitations as finite and sinful beings as well as an acknowledgment of the full humanity of others (in the positive sense as image-bearers).[29] In simple terms, Christian historians have no

---

27. Of course, later historians sometimes must legitimately revise the wrong interpretation of earlier scholars. For a brief discussion of the difference, see James McPherson, "Revisionist Historians," *Perspectives on History*, September 2003, accessed 18 February 2018, https://www .historians.org/publications-and-directories/perspectives-on-history/september-2003/revision-ist-historians. For an illustration from a popular source, see Justin Taylor, "What Is Revision-ist History?" *The Gospel Coalition Blog*, 7 July 2017, accessed 19 February 2018, https://www .thegospelcoalition.org/blogs/evangelical-history/what-is-revisionist-history/.

28. Although we do not believe the result of such dialogue is "objectivity," G. R. Evans describes something similar to this in her article, "Ecumenical Historical Method," *JES* 31 (1994): 93–110. She points out both benefits and pitfalls in such ecumenical historiography, which principles can apply to historiography in general (Marc Bloch, *The Historian's Craft*, trans. Peter Putnam [New York: Knopf, 1953], 69).

29. Hans Urs von Balthasar rightly argues that we as Christian historians cannot "lay down an unrelated 'double truth,' with the secular scholar and scientist on the one hand and the theologian on the other studying the same object without any encounter or intersection between their two methods. Nor, finally, can we allow the secular disciplines to be absorbed by theology

advantage over non-Christians in intelligence, skill, talent, or method, so they should read widely and study deeply. At the same time, they must also never forget to embody the virtues of integrity, discernment, wisdom, and humility.

❝ Taking Your Seat

C. S. Lewis once defined "chronological snobbery" as "the uncritical acceptance of the intellectual climate common to our own age and the assumption that whatever has gone out of date is on that account discredited."[30] Without looking back, you'll repeat the errors of the past and disinherit the successes of those believers who have gone before. Every reform movement in the history of the church was sparked and fueled by looking back at what had been lost in later generations. To forsake the deep roots of the Great Tradition of Christian biblical interpretation, application, theology, and ministry is to weaken the branches of our modern faith. We suggest gaining some familiarity with the saints who have gone before. Get some guidance from a pastor, teacher, mentor, or professor—then read widely and deeply. Observe how God has revealed his grace, mercy, justice, and providence throughout history. Learn from the way his Spirit has seen fit to preserve the body of Christ through good times and bad. Don't silence the voice of the Historian through neglect. Give voice to the Historian through diligence.

CONCLUSION

God's providence throughout human history is itself a nonverbal revelation of God, his works, and his ways. This includes especially the history of biblical interpretation, Christian living, doctrine, and practices. Pastors and teachers of the past should not be forgotten. Nor should they be worshipped.

The careful, critical, and cautious pursuit of the Historian will help Christians gain wisdom and insight from the unfolding of history.

---

as though it alone were competent in all cases because Christ alone is the norm" (Balthasar, *Theology of History*, 13–14).

30. C. S. Lewis, *Surprised by Joy: The Shape of My Early Life* (San Diego: Harcourt Brace & Company, 1955), 207–208.

The Historian's role in the Table conversation is to bring the past to life—to shine the light of past experiences on contemporary events and challenges, and to re-invite to the Table the often forgotten or forsaken voices of the saints of the past who still have much to teach us.

Jerusalem Council

The participants in the Jerusalem Council had a keen awareness of how historical events came to bear on their contemporary situation. As they sought how to apply the doctrinal principles to the matter of Gentile believers worshiping side-by-side with Jewish believers, they factored in the historical background to understand the cultural realities. James spoke with *the voice of the Historian* when he pointed out that "from ancient generations" Jews had been preaching the "law of Moses" in the synagogues (Acts 15:21, NASB). This observation added depth and perspective to the issue.

This history had resulted in a large representation of socially Jewish people accustomed to certain practices that made it difficult to fellowship with other Gentiles. The Jewish customs weren't just passing fads, the result of constantly changing cultural conditions. Had that been the case, it's unlikely the council would have been as concerned about them. Rather, the divisions between Jewish and Gentile cultural expectations had deep historical roots. Change would take a lot of time. An awareness of history was essential to make a proper diagnosis of the problem and to propose a proper prescription.

And let's not lose sight of the fact that the entire account of the Jerusalem Council—their methods and their findings—comes to us as a result of the diligent work of a particular historian, Luke. Like his Gospel, Luke's account in the book of Acts was a compilation of both eye-witness accounts and his own experiences, recorded after investigating "everything carefully" and written "in consecutive order" (Luke 1:3; Acts 1:1 NASB). Without the voice of the Historian, we would have no example of the Jerusalem Council at all!

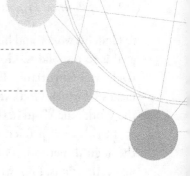

CHAPTER 12

INVITATION TO
THE TABLE

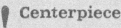

Centerpiece

All believers are invited to the task of theology: the discourse concerning God, his works, and his ways.

Some think that only professionals can do theology—paid professionals like Old or New Testament scholars, professors of theology, church historians, or ordained clergy. But anybody who encounters God's revelation and responds to it is doing theology.[1] In fact, it's impossible to live in the world God created without responding to him. Every breath we take is a gift from God and a response to his revelation. In the task of theology, then, we interact with others who are listening and responding to God's revelation—those who do so consciously or unconsciously.

To bring this inevitable response to God's revelation from the unconscious to the conscious, from the haphazard to the orderly, from the erratic to the consistent, from the hasty to the reflective—this is the purpose of developing theological method. All humans respond

---

1. Charles C. Ryrie, *Basic Theology: A Popular Systematic Guide to Understanding Biblical Truth* (Wheaton: Victor Books, 1986; reprint, Chicago: Moody, 1999), 9, writes, "Even an atheist has a theology. He thinks about God, rejects His existence, and expresses that sometimes in creed and always in lifestyle." It would be better to say "always in creed and sometimes in lifestyle," since "there is no god" is a creed.

to God, his works, and his ways—believers and unbelievers alike. Our goal is to respond to God's revelation carefully, critically, constructively, and Christianly. But first, we need to understand the various means by which God's revelation comes to us: through the Word to the World, the Word in the World, and the World of the Word.

In this brief primer, we've only begun to scratch the surface of theological method. The dimensions of doing theology extend in many directions. Even when we begin to develop some competency in its length and breadth (the topics and people involved) we'll still need to attend to its height and depth (the subtopics and sub-disciplines in each realm). Then, all of these dimensions extend into the past and continue into the future as we explore the history of doctrine from people of the past while keeping an eye on the questions and concerns of the future.

Feeling overwhelmed yet?

Perfect. This is just where we want you.

Because the truth is, *we can't do theology on our own.*

We were never meant to.

THEOLOGY IN COMMUNITY

In her primer on epistemology ("knowing-ology"), Esther Lightcap Meek characterizes the process of knowing as "joining a team of explorers who intend to venture together toward knowing."[2] She explains, "Reality proves to be richly multi-faceted. Working with others in our knowing venture, we can pool our diverse perspectives and training so that we can engage the world even more responsibly and effectively."[3]

The book of Proverbs asserts, "Where there is no guidance the people fall, but in abundance of counselors there is victory" (Prov. 11:14, NASB). Proverbs 1:5 presents the positive side of this: "A wise man will hear and increase in learning, and a man of understanding will acquire wise counsel" (NASB). The Hebrew word *tachbulah*, translated "guidance" and "counsel" in these proverbs, refers

---

2. Esther Lightcap Meek, *A Little Manual for Knowing* (Eugene OR: Cascade, 2014), 8.

3. Meek, *A Little Manual for Knowing*, 8.

to "deliberation," which implies contributions from more than one source of insight and learning.[4] Of course, bad counselors can lead to destruction (Prov. 12:5), but it's right and necessary to draw on the wisdom, guidance, and insight of others as we deliberate, consider, and weigh evidence and arguments. This is also true for theological method.

This is why we illustrate theological method with the metaphor of the Table. Obviously, the Table doesn't actually exist. But it could. And maybe it should. Probably never in the history of the church, though, did representatives from these various diverse perspectives and training sit down and have an open and honest—or even lively and passionate—discussion concerning God's threefold revelation. Maybe at times we've come close in councils, conventions, conferences, or colloquia. Nevertheless, the illustration of the Table serves as a reminder that we are meant to do theology in community, in real dependence on the knowledge, wisdom, and insights of others. And it gives us a concrete image of the kinds of interrelated, interdependent fields of labor that have contributed to our discourse concerning God, his works, and his ways throughout the history of Christian theology.

JERUSALEM COUNCIL: A BIBLICAL EXAMPLE OF THEOLOGY AT "THE TABLE"

The principle of Christians coming together in a council to deliberate over theological matters is exemplified in the Jerusalem Council in Acts 15. In the course of their gospel ministry to the Gentiles, Paul and Barnabas went toe-to-toe with certain Jewish followers of Jesus who were teaching, "Unless you are circumcised according to the custom of Moses, you cannot be saved" and "It is necessary to circumcise them [Gentiles] and to direct them to observe the Law of Moses" (Acts 15:1, 5, NASB). Great controversy erupted over this serious doctrinal issue regarding what is necessary for salvation, leading Paul and Barnabas to head to Jerusalem to consult with the "apostles and elders" there (15:2).

---

4. See entry in Ludwig Koehler et al., *The Hebrew and Aramaic Lexicon of the Old Testament* (Leiden: Brill, 2000), 1716.

In Acts 15:6, we read, "The apostles and the elders came together to look into this matter" (NASB). The issue was clearly doctrinal and practical: what must one do to be saved? The goal of the dialogue was to seek the truth of God's revelation concerning the matter. The method of seeking understanding was to come together and to debate (15:6–7). The word translated "debate" (*zētēsis*) doesn't necessarily indicate a mean-spirited fight; it can also mean an investigation or discussion.[5] Not only were the apostles involved in this deliberation, but so were the "elders"—other pastors and teachers of the church in Jerusalem.

When Peter himself stood up, he didn't shut down the discussion with a prophetic utterance from the Lord, but he offered an argument from their ministry experience of the Lord cleansing the hearts of the Gentile believers by faith (Acts 15:7–9). Here we see *the labor of the Minister* at work. Beyond this, Peter reaffirmed a core tenet of Christian teaching: "We believe that we are saved through the grace of the Lord Jesus" (15:11, NASB). Recall *the task of the Theologian*: aligning theology to core doctrines of the faith "once for all entrusted" to God's people (Jude 3). Paul and Barnabas also contributed to the discussion by relaying their own personal ministry experience of God working signs and wonders among the Gentiles (15:12)—the *labor of the Minister* represented again.

Next, James confirmed the theological conclusions Peter drew from experience by quoting Scripture: "Simeon has related how God first concerned Himself about taking from among the Gentiles a people for His name. With this the words of the Prophets agree, just as it is written" (15:14–15 NASB). James assumed *the role of the Interpreter* in reading and applying Scripture to the matter at hand.

Through this deliberation, the council had "become of one mind" (15:25, NASB), thus guided by virtues of love, unity, humility, and harmony. In this way, all members of the council bore *the burden of the Virtuous*. However, as they sought how to apply the doctrinal principle to the matter of Gentile believers living and worshiping side-by-side with Jewish believers, they also factored in both history and culture.

---

5. *See* William Arndt, Frederick W. Danker, and Walter Bauer, *A Greek-English Lexicon of the New Testament and Other Early Christian Literature*, 3d ed. (Chicago: University of Chicago Press, 2000), 428–29.

James noted that "from ancient generations," Jews had been preaching the "law of Moses" in major cities (15:21, NASB). Here James takes on *the voice of the Historian* to add depth and perspective to the issue.

This history had resulted in a large representation of socially Jewish people accustomed to certain practices that made it difficult to mix with people of other cultures. This is a recognition of what we know today as sociological and psychological issues—*the pursuit of the Scientist* in a primitive but nevertheless real form. This social consideration and the accompanying psychological effects on the community were weighed when limiting the freedom of Gentiles who were living with believing Jews in the church (15:19–21).

And what did they do when the council concluded their deliberation? Someone among them, skilled in the art of writing, crafted a letter on their behalf. The letter was written according to the prevailing cultural forms of the day (15:23–29). Here we see *the passion of the Artist* at work, crafting a culturally appropriate work to communicate and persuade readers of the truth. Finally, we shouldn't overlook the fact that the entire exercise involved careful arguments, evidence, logic, and reasoning—concrete manifestations of *the quest of the Philosopher.*

In this particular case, the dialogue involved apostles, pastors, and teachers—"the whole church" (15:22)—who met together and drew wisdom and insight from Holy Scripture, from personal and shared ministry experience, from core doctrines centered on the saving work of Jesus Christ, and even from historical and cultural realities. Weighing the evidence and arguments, they came to a consensus on the matter, settling the doctrinal and practical question. This is a great biblical example of a *community* approach to asking and answering theological questions. In this episode, we catch a glimpse of the Table method of theological discourse at work in the pages of Scripture itself.

CONCLUSION

As a Christian in a community—with relationships in the local church, global church, and historical church—you're already at the Table. You may not have been aware of it until now, but you're already doing theology. You've made doctrinal, practical, and moral decisions based on the Word to the World, the Word in the World, and the World of the Word. You've engaged in discourse with other believers (and unbelievers) regarding God, his works, and his ways. You've come to the metaphorical Table with interests and expertise to share with others—and with gaps and weaknesses in your own interests and expertise for others to supplement. Our hope is that this primer will help you determine your own place at the Table. And we hope that you might actually pull up a chair to a real table with other Christians, share a meal or coffee together, and experience the remarkable work of Christian theology.

- Are you filling the role of the Interpreter by providing vital guidance in biblical exegesis and biblical theology, maintaining the standard of inspired Scripture as the inviolable norming norm of theological method?
- Are you focusing on the task of the Theologian, guided by the "Rule of the Faith" as a confessional cornerstone and focusing on doctrinal standards believed, taught, and confessed in the body of Christ worldwide?
- Are you bearing the burden of the Virtuous, serving as the conscience of the Table by attending to virtues of faith, hope, love, prudence, temperance, fortitude, and justice as well as beauty, balance, and proportion?
- Are you representing the quest of the Philosopher by providing insight into fundamental questions of hermeneutics, truth, logic, worldview, and critical thinking necessary to better understand, defend, and articulate theology?
- Are you engaged in the pursuit of the Scientist, sharing your knowledge gained through the observation of natural phenomena, exploring God's self-revelation in creation to better understand and communicate theological truth?
- Are you reflecting the passion of the Artist, contributing through art and culture as a particular means of revealing the image of God through human creativity in order to better understand and articulate God, his works, and his ways?

- Are you primarily engaged in the labor of the Minister, contributing to theological reflection through practical Christian living and ministry to better understand God's revelation and more effectively communicate theological truth?
- Are you giving voice to the Historian by sharing wisdom and insight from unfolding human history under the providence of God as well as from pastors and teachers of the past?

Perhaps the Lord has called and gifted you to pull double—or even triple—duty. Maybe you have interests, training, and experience in areas that—until now—you didn't even realize were welcome at the Table. Maybe you have interests but need training, or training and need experience. Whatever your particular, unique situation, just remember...

The Table is set. Many invitees have already taken their seats. In fact, they've been chatting with each other for generations. Even centuries. But it's not too late to get involved. God's revelation is calling to us—to *all* of us, and to *each* of us. Men and women from every tongue, tribe, and nation, from every social group, economic background, political persuasion, and cultural heritage.

The Spirit of God is drawing you to the Table.

Please accept the invitation.

66 Taking Your Seat

We hope your understanding of theology has been affected by this book. It's not an academic discipline of the lone scholar with advanced degrees and a paid position. It's discourse between believers of every background, from anywhere in the world, and from every era of history, concerning God, his works, and his ways. We also hope your attitude toward theology has been changed by this book. It's not boring, irrelevant, theoretical rambling about esoteric ideas and incomprehensible concepts. It's a dynamic, edifying, exciting, and ongoing conversation. Sometimes as action-packed as a sporting event. Sometimes as exhilarating as an adventure. Sometimes subdued, like a dinnertime conversation or a chat over coffee. And we hope this book has motivated you to action—to get involved. Open books by people you don't know about things you don't understand. Dialogue with people from diverse perspectives who can give voice to areas of interest and expertise with which you're unfamiliar. And work together toward accomplishing God's mission of growing and going, knowing that one day the dim mirror of our partial understanding will give way to a fuller knowledge of God, his works, and his ways (1 Cor. 13:8–13).

SCRIPTURE INDEX

GENERAL INDEX

culture, 102, 108, 123, 124, 125,
126, 127, 128, 129, 131, 132,
144, 164
definition, 122
popular, 20, 119, 128, 129, 145
theological method and, 53
Culver, Robert Duncan, 49

D

Davies, G. I., 156
DeMoss, Matthew S., 13
Didache, 86
doctrinal statements, 82, 83, 152
dogmatic theology, *see* theology,
dogmatic
Dyer, John, 123
Dylan, Bob, 20
Dyrness, William A., 131

E

Eastern Orthodox Church, 77
economics philosophy, 104
economics, 104
ecumenical creeds, *see* creeds, ecumenical; church councils
Edwards, Jonathan, 12, 78
empiricism, 100
engineering, 20, 116, 123, 139
Enlightenment, 11, 100
epistemology, 19, 100, 102, 103,
104, 162
Erickson, Millard J., 86
ethics, 19, 95, 102, 103, 104, 108,
109, 120
Eucharist, *see* sacraments (ordinances), Lord's Supper
evangelical(ism), 11, 81, 137
Evans, G. R., 158
evil, problem of, 102

evolution, 112
exegesis, exegetes, 28, 29, 59, 66, 70,
84, 108, 109, 139, 166
experience, 39, 56, 69, 93, 107, 113,
121, 122, 135, 143, 146, 149,
164, 165

F

faith (*fide, pistis*)
objective content, 29, 31, 61, 73-74,
76, 83, 144, 146, 150, 152, 164
subjective belief, 6, 73-74, 144
fallacies
logical, 103, 109
rhetorical, 100, 109
Farrar, Frederic William, 147
film, 125, 129, 133
first-tier source of theology, *see*
source(s) of theology, first-tier
Fischer, John, 53
Franke, John R., 68
free will, 155

G

Galileo Galilei, 113, 119
general revelation, *see* revelation,
general
geology, 30
George, Timothy, 68
Getz, Gene, 137
gifts, spiritual, *see* Holy Spirit, gifts of
Gilkey, Langdon, 155
Glahn, Sandra, 153
God
attributes, 33, 39, 51, 52, 105, 112,
113, 125, 143, 155
Creator, 117, 123, 155
existence, 31, 85, 102, 143
the Father, 49, 74

theological method
  as an art, 30-31, 32
  Bible-only approach, 49
  biblical examples, 24, 35-36, 45,
    57, 71, 85, 98, 110, 121, 133-
    134, 146, 160, 163-165
  in community, 56, 167-168
  as a dialogue, 31, 32, 35-36, 44
  as a science, 30
  definition, 17, 25, 26, 31, 35
  description, 37
  disposition for, 90-91
  distinct from exegetical method, 28
  distinct from hermeneutics, 28
  eclectic, 32, 33
  goal, 34, 35
  hermeneutical, 31-32
  integrative, 32, 33
  revelation and, 38
  varieties of, 11
theology
  academic, 138
  anthropocentric, 76
  biblical, 27, 28, 70, 81
  bibliocentric, 77
  canonical, 27
  center of, 76
  christocentric, 50, 76, 77
  in community, 31, 45
  confessional, 81
  definitions, 25, 27, 31, 33, 59, 73
  as discourse, 22, 25, 26, 31, 33,
    38, 44
  dogmatic, 81
  ecclesiocentric, 77
  eschatocentric, 77
  as "faith seeking understanding,"
    19, 61, 73
  historical, 27, 42, 81, 139, 154

liberal, 77, 100, 139, 153
missional, 138
pastoral, 27
philosophical, 81
practical, 20, 81, 94, 134, 135,
  137, 138, 139, 167
second-tier dialogue, 37
as study of God, 25, 26, 37
systematic, 27, 28, 42, 81, 84,
  138, 139
theocentric, 76
Theophilus of Antioch, 105, 130
"Thirty-nine Articles of Religion",
  63
Thomas Aquinas, *see* Aquinas,
  Thomas
tradition(s), 32, 35, 81, 101, 124
  Great Tradition, *see* Great Tradi-
    tion, the
  positive, 147, 149, 151
  negative, 147, 150, 151
  neutral, 148
  traditio activa, 149
  traditio passiva, 149
Treier, Daniel J., 80-81
Trinitarian creation-fall-
  redemption narrative, 51, 55,
  64, 67, 74-75, 76, 77, 78-82, 85,
  96, 97, 125, 156-157
Trinity, 29, 49-50, 51, 52, 79-80, 82,
  85, 92, 107
Turner, Steve, 127

V

Van den Belt, Henk, 69
Vanhoozer, Kevin J., 60, 80-81, 137
Veeneman, Mary, 69
vice, 42, 86, 96, 97, 98, 124
Viladesau, Richard, 126